THE SUNDAY TIMES

Build Your Personal Brand

THIRD EDITION

D0807773

Eleri Sampson

KOGAN PAGE | *CREATING SUCCESS*

My special thanks to my family, friends, colleagues and clients for their interest and support and very special thanks to my partner Alan Felton.

First published in 1994 as *The Image Factor*
Second edition 1996
Third edition 2002

Kogan Page Limited
120 Pentonville Road
London N1 9JN

British Library Cataloguing in Publication Data

A CIP record for this book is available from the British Library

ISBN 0 7494 3851 7

Typeset by Jean Cussons Typesetting, Diss, Norfolk
Printed and bound in Great Britain by Clays Ltd, St Ives plc

contents

exercise: what really matters to me?

Jot down a few words and phrases in response to this question. Do any of your words appear in the list in Table 1.1? If not, add your own. Mark your top three choices.

Table 1.1

Authenticity – to be myself	Autonomy/independence
Challenge	Compassion
Competence: be really good at something	Entrepreneurial activity
Fairness	Family and friends
Financial reward	Freedom
Fun – have a good time	Health and fitness
Honesty	Integrity
Making a difference	Personal development
Power	Profit
Recognition	Stability/security
Status	Team working
Variety	

Suppose your top three choices are 'fun', 'integrity' and 'making a difference'. Do you know how you project these values to the world through the way you behave, what you wear, how you talk, how you do business and how you treat people? Would you say that people would recognise you as someone who enjoys what he/she is doing, is trustworthy, cannot be bribed or flattered, and is committed to developing his/her staff team? If so, then your values are showing on the outside in the form of your reputation and you are on the way to making fun, integrity and making a difference a recognisable, distinctive brand.

exercise: how do you want to come across? your public self

Jot down a few words and phrases in response to this question. Do any of your words appear in the list in Table 1.2? If not, add your own. Mark your top three choices.

Table 1.2

Affluent	Elegant	Reserved	Amusing
Efficient	Serious	Approachable	Fair
Stylish	Arty	Fashionable	Successful
Compassionate	Friendly	Talkative	Capable
Organised	Thoughtful	Confident	Professional
Well-educated	Creative	Relaxed	Well-mannered
Dynamic			

Suppose your top three choices are 'fashionable', 'professional' and 'organised'. Do you know how you project these values to the world through the way you behave, what you wear, how you talk, how you do business and how you treat people? Would you say that people would recognise you as someone who enjoys wearing the latest looks, is well informed about his/her specialism and keeps his/her correspondence and files in order? If so, then your values are showing on the outside in the form of your reputation and you are on the way to making fashionable, professional and organised a recognisable, distinctive brand.

how do you come across?

Ask yourself, 'How would I like to come across to the people I would most like to impress?' How do you think you really come across? Is there a gap? How do you know how you come across? We do not all have the gift of self-awareness. Most of us receive feedback in one form or another, formally through an appraisal maybe, or informally from a friend or colleague. So listen to the feedback. It can come in the form of compliment or criticism.

identify perception gaps

If you think you come across as fashionable but only wear fashionable clothes to clubs and parties, not work, that is a perception gap. If you think you come across as professional but gossip about clients, that is a perception gap. If you think you come across as organised but miss trains, arrive late for meetings, keep people waiting, that is a perception gap.

'Customers prefer conducting business with individuals who meet their visual expectations.' So says Jeff Mowatt, a Canadian expert on client service. 'First impressions may not be fair, but they are the realities of the business world. You hire employees to take care of customers, not for the sake of expressing their sartorial individuality. They can do that on their own time.' He cites several examples of the perception gap:

- The waitress with too much make up, sporting tattoos and with body piercing would likely put off a patron of an upmarket restaurant.
- A plumber in an Armani suit makes the client feel uncomfortable.
- The bar tender in conservative suit and tie may appal a customer in an alternative nightclub.

I know this is so obvious it is hardly worth mentioning, but sometimes it is useful to confront the obvious and see what it has to say to you. Your colleagues, clients, family and friends can tell you when they experience a perception gap, so ask them.

exercise: one small step

As a result of your honest analysis of your public self and how you come across, you may want to make some improvements. If you do, then take the 'one small step' approach. Construct a paragraph from the key words on your list, using these starter points for each sentence:

I'd like to appear more...
One aspect of this is...
If I want to address this aspect, I could...
This is my first step to appearing more...
Therefore it is also a first step to projecting my personal brand.

I'd like to appear less...
One aspect of this is...
If I want to address this aspect, I could...
This is my first step to appearing less...
Therefore it is also a first step to projecting my personal brand.

example
I would like to appear more organised. One aspect of this is that I can never find anything on my desk. If I want to address this aspect, I could buy some vertical storage holders because papers look less disorganised when they are filed upright rather than spread around flat. This is my first step to appearing more organised. Therefore it is also a first step to projecting my personal brand.

being brilliant is not enough

Have you noticed that being brilliant, being the best or even working extraordinarily hard are not enough to help you succeed in your career? In my job as an executive coach, I regularly meet people, brilliant people, who are not making the success of their careers that they hoped to or were expected to. What many of these people have in common is that they have not understood the extent to which their personal style is a contributing factor to their perceived (not necessarily their actual) value to their organisation or professional field. In other words, they have neglected to make their professional values visible through their personal style. They have an underdeveloped 'personal brand'. If this rings true for you, then as well as being competent at what you do, you will also need to develop your trademark: a consistent, distinctive and recognisable personal identity that is your 'personal brand'. The idea is that everything about you is an affirmation of the identity you have designed for yourself.

marketing yourself

Let us put branding into the general context of marketing. We are all familiar with marketing as a business activity, and branding is part of that activity. Every activity should support the core brand message. Most marketing experts would agree that there is a common core of elements in the practice of marketing. These core elements are usually referred to as the 'marketing mix'. My particular favourite mix comprises the following: product, price, place, packaging, perception and promotion plus a UPB (unique perceived benefit).

product

In the scenario we are building, the product is you: your values, experience, temperament and personality. It is also a combination of what you are good at, what you are bad at, what

Marketing, among other things, is about building product awareness. Apply this principle to yourself and inform people about what you stand for, what you have to offer and how to find you. The 'marketing mix' consists of:

- ▓ Product
- ▓ Price
- ▓ Place
- ▓ Packaging
- ▓ Promotion
- ▓ Perception
- ▓ plus your UPB…

…unique perceived benefit

reputation you have, who you know, what motivates you, what turns you off.

exercise: product description

Draw a box and divide it into four quadrants numbered 1–4.

Quadrant 1 is for you to write about your personal qualities: sentences that begin 'I can…'

Quadrant 2 is for you to write about your skills: sentences that begin 'I am…'

Quadrant 3 is for you to write about your experience: sentences that begin 'I have…'

Quadrant 4 is for you to write about your beliefs and convictions: sentences that begin 'I believe…'

example
Quadrant 1: I am a quiet, thoughtful person who likes generating lots of ideas. I am reliable and resourceful.

Quadrant 2: I can use a wide range of computer software to generate graphic designs. I can also speak French and Italian.

Quadrant 3: I have a degree in graphic design, an HGV licence, have worked in France and Italy and have 10 years' experience designing annual reports for blue-chip companies.

Quadrant 4: I believe in giving some of my professional services to charity.

identifying your special product features

If you now add 'so what?' to these statements you can start to evaluate them in the context of what is special and unusual, what is commonplace, and what needs to be revamped or added. For example, there are many graphic design graduates: but how many have worked in Italy and believe in giving some of their professional services to charity?

Then go on to make a sentence which includes 'I can…', 'I am…', 'I have…', 'I believe…', and closes with 'which means that…'. The whole sentence, even if a little unwieldy, will be a true snapshot of you and your values. You can construct as many 'special product features' as you need from the information in the four quadrants and shape them to your needs.

price

In this context, the price is what you are worth in the marketplace: the salary, fees, perks that you can command for what you do. If you are an expert, do you know what other experts in your field charge? Make sure you know the market rate for your job in the same or similar market sectors. It is up to you to keep yourself constantly up-to-date and well-informed. You need to review your role, job function and job description from time to time to check whether the price is right for the job.

place

This is the physical context of where you make, do or sell what you produce and your place of work. Place is also where your audience or your customer base is to be found. Your organisation, department, project team, your clients, colleagues and competitors are your marketplace for your branded product. Individuals are usually happiest when they can work in a business environment that is in harmony with their values. One way of looking at this is to look at the organisational culture of the company.

Two contrasting examples of organisational culture could be:

Conservative	Creative
■ The traditional way	■ Innovative
■ Status quo	■ Changing
■ Rule-bound	■ Free structure
■ Old-fashioned	■ New
■ Slow	■ Fast
■ Autocratic	■ Democratic

The world of work also presents different kinds of business orientation. There is a sophisticated mix between the way an organisation conducts its business and the nature of its business. Broadly speaking, as well as taking into account a company's organisational culture, it is useful to identify its business orientation. Most businesses are orientated in one of four directions:

- ■ projects: for example architectural practices, software applications;
- ■ processes: for example, factories producing goods or parts;

- ▓ people: service industries, entertainment, PR;
- ▓ ideas: for example product design, advertising.

Some organisations are so huge that they represent the whole range of orientations across their departments and functions. The trick is to look for a good match between your values and the business orientation of the organisation.

packaging

We believe what we see. In a society ruled by visual images we are inclined to believe the evidence of our eyes. If someone looks professional we are prepared to believe them until they let us down. Packaging is how you express your personality. Appearances do count. You are what you wear. Clichés, I know, but true nevertheless. We make snap decisions based on what we see and cling to those decisions. This means packaging our best qualities so that they are projected through what we wear. An appropriate business wardrobe is a vital component of your personal brand. Details of personal appearance do matter, and make a strong contribution to the total effect of your personal brand. The way you package yourself through your image and professional persona is like an advertisement: it works in the same way as a coloured brochure or a flier or a Web page.

The image of the worker is sometimes dictated by the nature of the work, and therefore there are limited image choices. For example, a nuclear researcher requires protective clothing, a police officer requires a readily identifiable uniform, and a funeral director requires a sober suit. In the absence of a formal dress code, employees can usually sense what is acceptable within the organisation's culture. If it is important to you to get it right, you will need to look hard at the image of the successful and respected people. Ask yourself whether you can emulate it, whether there are compromises to be made, and if so, whether you can live with them. In the world of work it is actually very easy to slip on an appropriate corporate persona, or even several personae to match corporate or client expectations. The question is, what is in it for you?

exercise: required image

Do you know what the required image is within your business, your industry, your specialism, your profession or your organisation? Are there certain expectations that you are aware of and need to take note of? Is there a dress code where you work? If so, who takes notice of it and who ignores it?

perception

Perception is reality. People will judge you on how you come across. How you seem is all you will be, so you need to take steps to influence the perceptions of people with no previous knowledge of you and no information other than what is in front of them. In this context 'perception' refers to external perceptions of the value and purpose of your role and function, your specialism, and your professional standing. If you are familiar with Cadbury's Milk Tray chocolates and Godiva hand-made truffles you will have clearly defined perceptions of each. An example of a clash of perceptions comes from a finance director who was on a small but high level working party. He thought he was there for his ability to number crunch, but his CEO made it clear after a few false starts that he was there to talk opera to the Chairman.

exercise: gaining an insight

Sometimes an insight can come from a formal appraisal at work, or as a result of a 360 degree feedback exercise, or as a result of candid remarks from your boss or peer group. If you are still unsure about how you might be perceived by other people, try this:

- Invite a trusted friend, colleague or family member to join you for this exercise.
- Ask that person to write down your name in the middle of a piece of paper.
- Then ask him or her to jot down anything that comes to mind when they think of you. Try not to prompt him/her.
- Ask the person this question: 'What special job would you ask me to do that you know I am the best person for?'
- Share the results and say thank you. You do not have to enter into a debate or defend yourself if you do not want to. In fact it might be useful to take the information away and ponder on it quietly.
- Remember that whatever the person comes up with, it is only his or her point of view. Every description has its positive and negative interpretation. Any good quality over-played can become a liability.

promotion

Every product benefits from a marketing campaign that draws attention to its existence, because, to borrow from sales and marketing language, 'You won't buy it if you can't see it.' Promotion techniques are about building awareness so that people know who you are, what you stand for, what you have to offer and how to find you. Every product needs a marketing campaign so that people are made aware of its existence, so a sensible step to managing your own promotion is to design a visibility campaign. How visible is your role at work? How many people see you? How influential are they? How can you influence them? Is your work project based or people based? A subtly crafted self-marketing campaign positions you where you can be noticed.

For the sake of your own self-esteem, if nothing else, you need people to know when you are doing a good job, especially those who can help you to promote yourself.

Dorothy Leeds, *Marketing Yourself: How to sell yourself and get the jobs you've always wanted*

reputation

Reputation is an offshoot from promotion. People often make judgements about you before they have met you because your reputation has gone before you. This can work to your advantage or not. Judgements may be based on gossip, on generalities or specifics. 'Architects are a funny lot', 'Consultants are so difficult to work with, they're so arrogant', 'Anyone who trained at the Royal College of Music must be good'. Suppose you have developed a reputation for being fussy about the presentation of letters and reports: then people are likely to check their work more carefully before letting you see it. If you are an external consultant and have a reputation for being expensive but worth every penny, then new clients know to expect a high fee but get value for money. In a 'soft' organisation, someone who is prepared to hire and fire ruthlessly in order to maintain a high quality of service can acquire the reputation of a 'hatchet man' and be despised or feared. In a more macho organisation, the same quality of ruthlessness could be admired and respected.

UPB: unique perceived benefit

What have you got that your colleagues or competitors do not have? This is often the hardest question to answer, but well worth the effort. 'Unique' could mean being:

- ▨ the first;
- ▨ the best;
- ▨ the only;
- ▨ the cheapest;

- the most expensive;
- the most amusing.

'Unique' could mean having unexpected opposites in your life or career:

- having breadth <u>and</u> depth of experience;
- qualifications in art <u>and</u> science;
- having worked at home <u>and</u> abroad.

'Unique' could be used to mean 'unusual':

- came up the hard way;
- shifted your career or specialism;
- broke away from family traditions or expectations;
- struggled against demons, dragons or deprivation.

'Unique' could also take the form of a shopping list: an impressive list of qualifications, successful, projects, publications, clients.

exercise: personal brand statement

The unique way that you combine the elements of image, personality, skills, experience and values is your personal brand.

Create a 10-word statement about yourself.

Create a 30-second sound bite about yourself.

exercise: personal evaluation

- What do I stand for?
- What am I known for?
- How can I stand out?
- How do I add value?
- What is my visibility rating? (international, national, regional, local, internal, departmental?)

the 'identity mix': the external elements of your personal brand

■ **Appearance:** how you look and what you wear, your level of personal maintenance, grooming, your standard of clothes maintenance, health and fitness.

■ **Voice:** how you sound, your tone of voice and the way you speak, your accent and pace of speech.

■ **Body language:** the way you sit and stand, the way you walk and move, your facial expression, your gestures, eye contact.

■ **Listening:** your level of listening skills and how you demonstrate the quality of your listening through body language.

■ **Verbal messages:** the content of what you have to say, how you express yourself, the range of language you use, your vocabulary, how you describe and publicise what you do and what you stand for.

■ **Presence and impact:** the way you project yourself to other people, your status, your level of confidence, authority, sophistication, attitude, your behaviour within and outside the organisation.

■ **Extended brand image:** people, places, things and ideas, philosophies that you associate with, the environment or physical context of where you work. We all surround ourselves with our particular tools of the trade: laptop, Rotring pen, colour swatches, card samples, stethoscope and so on. We also extend our image by association, and rather like having bridesmaids at a wedding we display our wealth, taste and style through our choice of unnecessary props and accessories which we hope will contribute to our standing in the organisation, our status or self-esteem.

The inner and outward elements (values plus image) of your 'personal brand' are complex and interlinked and should be seamlessly presented. In an ideal world your brand will match your business and career path.

image.impact.behaviour.communication.reputation.values.

Your marketing opportunity is to identify, then package and promote your UPB. My aim is to help you to recognise your personal and professional values, who you are and what you can contribute, and use this knowledge to develop your personal brand. This will put you in an advantageous position to market yourself subtly but with honesty, energy and conviction. Living your values is the key to a successful personal brand. To this end I have focused on packaging: how you package your values and demonstrate them through your image, impact and personal presentation.

are there any exceptions?

■ When you are paraded because of your connections.
■ When you are needed because of your skills.
■ When you are wanted because of your knowledge.

who can afford to ignore the rules?

■ The very powerful.
■ The very beautiful.
■ The very rich, who have nothing to prove.
■ The destitute, who have nothing to lose.

build your personal brand through effective communication

> So far as other people are concerned you are
> your behaviour. Although there are other things
> which go towards making you the person you
> are – your thoughts, feelings, attitudes, motives,
> beliefs and so on – your behaviour is apparent
> to everyone.
>
> Dr Peter Honey, psychologist and specialist in
> interactive skills

Communication can be defined as the transfer of thoughts, ideas and feelings through speaking, listening, writing, actions, behaviour, attitude, pictures, signs and symbols. Effective communication is clear, concise and accurate. Communicating your personal brand should follow the same rules. Your message of competence and confidence as a professional should be clearly communicated every day of your working life. Every message needs a medium to carry it – in this case your image is the medium that carries the message of your goals and ambitions, your abilities and what you stand for. In this chapter the emphasis is on non-verbal forms of communication.

How do you come across? Your early social conditioning, your background, experience of life, your education and genetic inheritance all contribute to your view of yourself and to your attitude to the world. These internal elements are externalised through:

- ▨ the way you behave with other people;
- ▨ the image you project;
- ▨ the values you hold;
- ▨ your communication style;
- ▨ the kind of language and vocabulary you use;
- ▨ your total impact, the sum of all of the above that others respond to.

first impressions and the power of non-verbal communication

Research by social psychologist Albert Mehabrian shows that more than 50 per cent of first impressions, out of context and with no background information, is based on the non-verbal which includes appearance, clothes and posture.

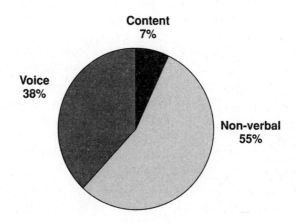

There are many aspects to non-verbal communication. These are the ones we notice when we meet other people:

- style of clothes;
- choice of colour;
- level of grooming;
- level of clothes maintenance;
- tone of voice;
- listening style;
- eye contact;
- facial expression;
- smile;
- posture;
- stance;
- gait;
- gestures;
- mannerisms.

Research shows that we do not have long to make the right impression. First impressions are powerful and lasting. A strong impression is made within moments and a lasting opinion based on how we look, sound and move within half a minute to four minutes. Few of us are free from irrational prejudice: men with beards, women in trousers, the Welsh, the Irish and so on. The initial impact is created by the way we look, the way we move and the way we sound, as well as what we have to say. Our perception of strangers is dominated by what we see, so we focus on their size and shape, dress, grooming, gestures and facial expression. Next we focus on what we can hear: things such as the tone of their voice, their accent and how loudly they speak. Finally we focus on the words themselves.

We process this information in order to get ready to meet what we presume is going to be a certain kind of person. We try to interpret the signals against our own knowledge, experience and prejudice. We absorb, then edit the information we receive, sometimes for its own sake, usually for practical reasons. The material is used to help us to define the situation. We ask ourselves questions such as, is this person potentially safe or dangerous? What behaviour will be needed from me? What kind of behaviour can I expect from the other person?

We are led to believe that judgements are made within minutes. Indeed they are, but not by everyone. It takes some people longer than others to sum up a stranger. Physical characteristics are then deduced, not always accurately. Our first impressions of each other are strongly influenced by our physical appearance and non-verbal behaviour. Some people have difficulty reading these non-verbal cues. Some of us use our intuition; others rely on the facts as they see them, weighing up the evidence before reaching a conclusion. This can take time: not just minutes but weeks or months. In many situations we do not know how much time it will take for other people to make judgements about us, so it is as well to try to make a good impression first time round.

impression management

In his important work *The Presentation of Self in Everyday Life*, American social psychologist Erving Goffman shows that we present ourselves to the world in two ways. First, *subconsciously*, we do things without our knowing it: for example, we might avoid eye contact with someone we are afraid of, or turn our body away from someone we do not like. Second, *consciously*, we make an effort to control our image by controlling our dress, body language and speech.

Goffman refers to this as 'dramaturgical control'. Like an actor, we costume and script our performance for the outside world in a considered way: for example, for a panel interview we might wear a suit, be especially careful about our grooming and adopt a rather formal manner. He calls this activity 'impression management', and this is the recurring theme in building your personal brand. We learn to manage the impression we create because we know it will influence how we are treated by other people. It does not mean we have to be false. Like a diamond, we polish and prepare ourselves and present different facets of ourselves to the world.

First impressions are based on what we see and are formed within minutes of meeting. We base our impressions on:

- Race
- Gender
- Age
- The way we look
- The way we move
- The way we sound
- Levels of attractiveness, success, sophistication, education, confidence, competence, authority, seniority
- Personality & temperament
- Up-bringing
- Financial status
- Social standing

the language of clothes

The language of clothes is formed from signs and symbols like any other language. Its vocabulary is formed from clothes, accessories and all kinds of personal decoration. 'Long before I am near enough to talk to you on the street, in a meeting or at a party, you announce your sex, age and class to me through what you are wearing – and very possibly give me important information (or misinformation) as to your occupation, origin, personality, opinions, tastes, sexual desires and current mood. By the time we meet and converse, we have already spoken to each other in an older and more universal tongue'. So said Alison Lurie, the American novelist and journalist, who popularised the concept of communication through dress in *The Language of Clothes* (first edition, 1982).

Articles of clothing have always had individual significance as signals of personal identity and acted as potent symbols of their time throughout the ages, from generation to generation and from culture to culture. They have the ability to speak clearly to those who have taken the trouble to learn the language. Every decade this century has an item of clothing that speaks for that decade and its social, political, economic and technological state. The short straight dresses worn by flappers in the 1920s tell of the physical and social emancipation of women. The flowers, soft lines and droopy fabrics worn by the hippies of the 1970s scream of the social trend to abhor war and return to nature. If clothes can reveal the truth, they can also tell lies. They can provide a disguise, reveal secrets or hide inadequacies. Whole outfits or even a single object can have different meanings.

Take the earring. In the 1980s the large gold earring was an obligatory accessory for a successful career woman. My mother's generation thought large gold earrings a vulgar display because small, discreet and probably pearl earrings only were worn with dressy clothes, after lunchtime. The sparkly stuff was saved for evening wear. My grandmother thought that having your ears pierced was 'common' and only for gypsies. She didn't think much of Queen Alexandra who had her ears pierced as a child, as was the Continental custom, and wore long, dangly earrings and a pearl choker, which became her personal style statement. Men who wore a single gold hoop in the time of Elizabeth I were pirates and adventurers, such as Sir Francis Drake. Today, a single good hoop might be worn by a gay man on one ear only, clusters of hoops are worn by punks, rich young footballers wear them in pairs – and they are shunned by fashionable women in favour of ethnic silver and beads.

A person's ability to understand the language of clothes is determined by several factors:

- ■ the level of their clothing awareness;
- ■ their level of interest in clothes;
- ■ their familiarity with the range of alternative interpretations;
- ■ their willingness to talk about clothes.

Colin McDowell robustly defends clothing as social comment in *Dressed to Kill: Sex, Power and Clothes* (1992), a densely written book that is neither social history, anthropological study nor fashion commentary but includes elements of each in the author's discursive style. He argues the case for a renewal of intelligent interest in clothing which has long been '...pushed aside by the majority of society'. He regrets the relegation of clothing in the form of fashion to a kind of ghetto visited only by fashion writers, eccentrics or the absurdly rich.

Whether you understand the nuances or not, body and clothes speak before you do. The conscious or unconscious visual image that is created through clothes is what we notice first. The picture that is formed by body, posture and dress speak to us before a word is uttered. We filter this visual information through our own experiences and preoccupations. When someone dresses in a style that closely mirrors our own we infer that they probably have similar attitudes, beliefs and values. We will probably be attracted to them and be more inclined to do business with them.

business casual

The shift away from formal business wear to casual clothes for business reflects the Californian influence – part Hollywood, part Silicon Valley – where not wearing a suit is a sign of success. In the UK, footballers and their wives, television presenters, media and dot.com entrepreneurs influence style by contributing glamour and informality. There are other influencing factors:

■ Working from home, teleworking for a company or working for yourself from your spare room means you could spend all week in your pyjamas if you wanted to.

■ The strong desire for individualism prevalent throughout the last two decades means that any inter-

ference with personal style is perceived as an infringement of human rights.

▨ The emphasis on knowledge and high-level technical
ability means these are valued, therefore rewarded,
more than interpersonal skills and appearance.

▨ In a more litigious society, if there is no explicit dress
code in place, there is an inclination to interpret
personal remarks or directives about personal behaviour or appearance as harassment.

▨ The spread and acknowledgement of cultural diversity
means people do not want to punish or exclude
cultural difference, or unfairly discriminate against it.

When the economy is good, people loosen up, but because we
are at the beginning of an economic downturn we are also at
the beginning of a return to formal dressing. However, casual
dress for business has become so deeply entrenched in some
organisations in the UK that there will not be overnight
changes.

character cues

There are many opportunities to transmit messages about character and style through a clever choice of clothing. When
clothes are used to define character they become a 'trade mark'
in the best sense of the word. I use a warm up exercise at semi-
nars called 'Who am I?' The point of the exercise is for delegates to find out as much as possible about each other without
asking any questions – to pick up any character cues they can.
They have to discover the age, interests and lifestyle of their
colleagues through observation and deduction rather than
verbal questioning. All the information they need is available
from dress and demeanour. Some find this exercise threatening.
They feel that they will reveal too much about themselves
through their observations – their lack of sophistication or

their lack of experience at reading the signals and making sense of them, or the chance that they might embarrass someone with a tactless remark. Others are almost clairvoyant in the accuracy of their interpretation. When people introduce themselves we look at the discrepancies between their 'truth' and ours. At this stage we discover our individual levels of fluency in reading the language of clothes.

This exercise parallels people's familiarity with a foreign language. In any group one or two will need an interpreter. Their low level of understanding can spring from a sense of intellectual superiority. They are really saying. 'There is no need to understand about clothes because words and ideas are more important'. Some discover they can do little more with the language of clothes than the equivalent of ordering a cup of coffee in French. They can tell the difference between smart and scruffy, classic or avant-garde but nothing more complex. Their sheltered upbringing, conservative background or low motivation has limited their opportunities to learn the necessary vocabulary. Others find they can read the language but not speak it. They pick up accurate signals from other people but are not able to experiment 'out loud'. They have internalised and intellectualised the process and are unwilling to put it to the test in a practical way. I have also noticed a minority who wear all the right things but can't explain how they arrived at their choice. They have the ability to mimic without understanding. Yet others have a large vocabulary, lots of confidence and the guts to try new things and learn from their mistakes.

There is a difference in the way men and women respond to this exercise. Some men use the opportunity to attack or undermine a colleague. Many men feel that talking about clothes is trivial – women's talk. They are filled with paranoia when aspects of dress are discussed. Both men and women under-estimate the social and political statements that clothes are capable of making. They fail to understand the link between appearance and personal identity. Fashion commentators continue to promote the notion that serious discussion about clothing should be at the centre of our interest in human behaviour. There is not yet a universal acceptance of this notion.

body language and presence

Body language – the bodily gestures, postures and facial expressions by which a person communicates non-verbally with others.

The American Heritage Dictionary of the English Language

non-verbal communication

The study of non-verbal communication, particularly through body language, is a comparatively new discipline, although the subject itself, of course, is not. From anthropologists to semiologists, academics only began to study this form of human communication from a scientific point of view in the 20th century. The notion that 'your body doesn't know how to lie' was popularised by Julius Fast in his book *Body Language* in 1970. Despite his warnings to be careful about oversimplifying the extent to which we can read true attitudes and feelings from body movement and gesture, we still like to believe we can do so.

Body language is a two-way street. It lets you know at an instinctive level what other people are thinking and feeling, and also conveys your thoughts and feelings to them. Two distinct kinds of messages can be conveyed non-verbally. First, gestures can replace words in the form of mime, as when you wave goodbye, and second, they can be involuntary gestures that express thoughts or feelings, as when you cover up your eyes at a road accident, meaning, 'I can't bear to look at it'.

Communicating personal style through body language is not

about projecting the right or wrong message or giving away hidden thoughts and feelings. It is more to do with using information about gesture and mannerisms and so on to project a positive image of oneself and to be more sensitive to the nonverbal signals of others. We can all brush up our people-reading skills by looking to really see and listening to really hear. The way they move their body can show how much a person is in control of a situation, can create a strong style signature and can have naturalness or falseness. In difficult situations, nerves can inhibit natural behaviour. People ask for advice about the right way to sit at an interview. 'Should I cross my legs? Should I lean forward or sit back? What will people think if I scratch my nose?' They worry that they will somehow be caught out. Learn to sit still, breathe properly, think positively and try to behave naturally is still the best possible advice.

Body language is a two-way street. It lets you know at an instinctive level what other people are thinking and feeling and also conveys your thoughts and feelings to them. Confidence or the lack of it is easily interpreted non-verbally.

Confident	Unsure
▓ Stillness	▓ Nervous mannerisms
▓ Eye contact	▓ Lowered gaze
▓ Easy stance	▓ Pacing about
▓ Using your space	▓ Hunched posture
▓ Expressive hands	▓ Fidgeting

professional presence

A professional demeanour will take into account the following aspects of body language:

Eyes. The ability to make and maintain eye contact looks confident; lowering the eyes appears submissive.

Face. Facial expression can show seven basic emotions: fear, anger, surprise, disgust, happiness, sadness, pain.

It's as well to know how your face registers these emotions and whether there is a chance that they might be misunderstood. Do you know whether you have expressive features or whether your face remains a mask whatever you are feeling?

Eyebrow flash. Raising the eyebrows for a few seconds when you catch someone's eye is friendly and reassuring. Try to respond to another's eyebrow flash unless you wish to signal disapproval or hostility.

Looking down your nose. If you hold your head up and tipped slightly back when looking at someone without bringing your head forward, you appear to be looking down your nose at them and come across as aloof or superior.

Posture. The way you sit, stand and walk can make you seem confident or timid, well or ill. The stance of a soldier on parade is not necessarily good posture. To achieve a confident and upright posture, imagine a piece of string threaded through your spine, up the back of your neck and out through the top of your head. When this string is pulled gently from above it gradually lifts and straightens the chest, shoulders and head. Imagine a helium balloon tied to this piece of string that will keep your head floating above your neck.

Gesture. Gestures such as handshaking, hugging, kissing or waving are conscious actions. Others, such as ear pulling, neck scratching or paper clip destruction are done unconsciously. We use gesture to emphasise the spoken word. Gestures should draw attention to the idea or shade of meaning, and not the gesture. They are also used when listening or being passive and can be warm or cold, aggressive, submissive, decorative or entirely unnecessary. Any attempt to interpret gesture should take into account:

▓ the *context* in which it's viewed – crossing arms and legs and hugging oneself can indicate a high level of insecurity, on a windy station platform it indicates trying to keep warm;

▓ the predominant *culture* – the meaning of hand gestures can vary considerably across cultures and continents;

▓ what other gestures are being used at the same time – try to interpret *clusters* of gestures rather than an isolated gesture.

Territory and positioning. Our sense of personal space is very important to us. We are all aware of our invisible defensive personal zone or 'space bubble'. The comfortable distance we can put up with will vary across cultures. There are city zones and country zones. We are sensitive to the distance between people and judge their relationships accordingly. Experts agree that four zones operate in Western culture.

personal zones

Acceptable distances between people vary with different social and personal situations:

▓ Intimate (0–0.45m) only entered with permission, otherwise can seem violent or hostile

▓ Personal
  - close personal (0.45–0.75m) eg for close friends, partner and family, friendly social gatherings
  - far personal (0.75–1.2m) eg at social gatherings where the atmosphere is slightly more formal

▓ Social (1.2–3.6m) eg across a room or piece of furniture, seminar leader and delegates

▓ Public (over 3.6m) eg speaker addressing a public meeting in a hall

touch

Touching at work is a sensitive issue. Warm, friendly people who instinctively touch as they talk can embarrass the cooler types. Touch can be interpreted as condescending – a pat on the head is what you give a child. Touch can be interpreted as sexual harassment – what you intended as a friendly gesture could be perceived as an uninvited sexual advance. Touch is therefore limited to the business handshake only unless there is an emergency or you want to offer support to a colleague in extreme physical or emotional crisis.

Levels of touch
Medical treatment – from a nurse or doctor to a patient.
Social – professional colleague handshake.
Friendship – hug and kiss to special friends not business acquaintances.
Love – close family only who are able to expose and respond to vulnerability.
Erotic – sexual arousal.

Business handshake. It is vital to have a good handshake, a powerful form of non-verbal introduction. Make it a clear statement of who you are, your status and intentions. Make sure you can go into your 'smile – eye-contact – handshake' routine confidently whenever it is appropriate. Women who are not used to this routine should practise it, as it is now expected that women will shake hands. They are expected to use less pressure than men.

A skilled people-reader can... work out most things about someone from the non-verbals they throw off on the 10 second flight path from door to desk.

Peter York, management consultant,
Management Today, 1999

Your handshake acts as your introduction before you say your name or give out your business card – and says more about you than either.

▓ **The Knuckle crusher** – the 'real man's' handshake – a firm, crunch-like grip may be compensating for the lack of something.

▓ **The two-hander** (or 'the glove'), the politician's handshake, patronising and insincere

▓ **The dead fish** – limp and damp, the loser's handshake

▓ **The right one** – for men and women – dry palm, soft skin, firm, palm-to-palm grip, web-to-web, hold for 2–3 seconds, elbow nearly straight, arm at right angles to the body, stand up, eye contact, smile

exercise

Try out your handshake on friends. Note what they say.

Mannerisms. Some common mannerisms can be interpreted like this:

▓ tilting the head sideways:
   – either shows interest in what's being said; or
   – could be a sexually submissive gesture like offering a vulnerable neck to a vampire; or
   – could be a signal of giving up.
▓ picking imaginary fluff can indicate boredom:
   – either your mind is elsewhere; or
   – you feel disagreement that you are not voicing.
▓ rubbing hands together quickly usually communicates enthusiasm and energy, eagerness to get on with the job, but it can look gauche or over-eager;
▓ patting hair, checking make-up, picking at cuticles all suggest lack of confidence. The only people who have constantly to check their appearance are models because they earn their living by it.
▓ hands in pockets:

- can look slovenly; or
- powerful, depending on the accompanying posture.

Putting your hands in jacket or trouser pocket or one hand in a side pocket as you get up to speak, and standing square to your audience feet apart, can look reassuring and business-like.

exercise

When watching TV, look at the newscaster or soap opera actors and analyse how much their facial expression supports or negates their message. Look particularly in the strong emotional or dramatic scenes.

your vocal image

Customers don't want to strain themselves to understand front line staff. If you or other employees don't speak the local language clearly, then customers will generally go to your competitors where they won't have to work so hard to communicate – or to spend money. This is doubly important when speaking on the telephone, where customers don't have the benefit of non-verbal communication to help them interpret what's being said.

This concept has nothing to do with discrimination based on ethnic differences or nationality. It has to do with basic communication skills that are essential to the job.

Jeff Mowatt, a Canadian expert on client service

The vocal impact you create when you speak is based on how people hear the individual quality of your voice. They hear the following:

- your delivery style, light and shade >> monotonous;
- your accent: local, regional, unidentifiable;
- the volume of your voice, loud >> soft;
- the pitch of your voice, low >> high;
- the pace of your speech, fast >> slow;

- your diction, clear >> mumbling;
- your breathing, laboured >> easy.

One of the rules of effective verbal communication is that people listen better when you make it easy for them to hear. Here are some basic rules:

- **Repetition:** repeat key words several times.
- **Involvement:** talk to, not at; ask questions.
- **Personal interest:** use names, mention interests.
- **Primacy and recency:** people tend to remember what they hear at the beginning and at the end of a presentation or conversation.
- **Demonstration:** do it or act it instead of talking about it.
- **Use props:** show an object as well as describing it.
- **Action:** hand gestures or body movement help to add emphasis to the words.
- **Vocal tone:** vary your tone of voice to add interest and avoid boredom.

reputation and visibility

Most of us are invisible. We have a small infrastructure of people who know us – our friends and family, people we meet at work, at church, at the golf club or sports centre, our neighbours and local shopkeepers – probably no more than a hundred or so people. Compared to international figures in politics, films and pop music most of us have a low level of 'well-known-ness'.

Recent research across a large number of organisations shows that there are three factors determining whether someone is promoted or not. The most influential factor is visibility or exposure. The contributing factors are made up in this way:

1. Doing the job – 10 per cent – your performance rating and how good you really are at your job and its tasks and responsibilities.
2. Image and personal style – 30 per cent – how you come across, your way of getting things done, your attitude. If these don't fit – you don't get the job.
3. Exposure and visibility – 60 per cent – who knows you, what kind of reputation you have, your contacts and published achievements.

If everyone in the organisation works hard, then image and visibility are more of an issue than performance.

One of the reasons why extremely able people fail to make

Figure 2.1 *Reputation and visibility*
Thank you to the 'Springboard' organisation and the cartoonist Viv Quillan.

their mark on a job or in an organisation is that they give the wrong impression. They come across as being disorganised or lacking ambition, or are reticent about their interest in a high profile project. We all know able people who have been over-looked because they simply have not stated their interest in promotion. Another reason is that the contribution they are making, albeit consistently and well, is simply not on the agenda. Early in my teaching career, I ran an Arts and Fashion Department in a local adult college. I thought my role was to develop and safeguard local centres of excellence. My boss thought I was there to promote the 'bread and butter' popular courses that would subsidise the esoteric or socially worthy courses that other departments found difficult to fund. Decisions about resources were a continual mystery to me and my profile remained low as did the internal status of my department. You may have experienced decisions that seem to you to be extraordinarily wilful or illogical. If that's the case it's time to check the agenda.

exercise

Write down what you think your job is and what you think you are actually achieving in that role. Ask your immediate boss what they think you are supposed to be doing in the job and what contribution they think you make to the department/organisation. Compare notes. The discrepancy can be astounding.

ten ways to promote yourself and increase your visibility

The workshops I run always have a session on designing self-marketing tactics and strategies. Every group comes up with good ideas. Here are some of them:

1. *Be well presented*

- Project an appropriate and positive professional image.
- Be consistently well-dressed and well-groomed. It has a doubly-positive effect – making you feel good as well as promoting a positive response from others.

2. *Be well informed*
- About the organisation.
- About your role and function.
- About your specialism. Make sure you are up to date. Opinions can change, knowledge advances. Fashions in management theory can change as rapidly as street fashion.

3. *Volunteer*
- Volunteer to do the kind of task that brings you to people's notice in a medium to large gathering, especially if there are going to be 'influencers' present.
- Organise a seminar.
- Deliver the report-back from small group discussions.
- Chair a working party.
- Make a speech at a retirement or leaving party.

4. *Get into print*
- Get used to the idea of publishing what you do. This is particularly important if you have a job with relatively low visibility. You must highlight your achievements in other ways.
- Try a short weekly report to your immediate line-manager, The Chief Executive or Chairperson.
- Contribute to specialist journals.
- Contribute to the in-house newsletter.
- Write up a report on courses attended.
- Write to say thank you to whoever funded your attendance on a course. Tell them what you got out of it and how you will use it in your

work.

- Organise tasks with your name on to be done in your absence. While you are away you are invisible.

5. *Effective networking*
   - Learn the skills of effective networking.
   - Use your contacts inside and outside the organisation.
   - Join appropriate associations and support groups *and go to the meetings*!

6. *Business cards*
   - Make sure you always have a supply of business cards with you. Public sector organisation's don't always provide cards so fund this yourself if necessary. 'Stickies' with your name and address on won't do.

7. *Photographs*
   - Have a set of professional black and white photographs taken. Use them for internal or external PR, for conference programmes when you are invited to speak and to accompany articles for professional journals.

8. *Make a good presentation*
   - Check out your presentation skills. Even if presentation is your business you need to update your style now and again. Everyone can get stale or develop bad habits.
   - Informal gatherings of colleagues can be a theatre for you to try out a new presentation style or newly acquired presentation skills.
   - Go on a good presentation skills course. Fund it yourself if necessary.
   - Present a report orally as well as writing it – a well presented report or a contribution to a meeting that is intelligent, concise and interesting will get you remembered. This is particularly

effective if the general standard of presentation at meetings is low.
- Learn to speak well on your feet in any circumstances.

9. *Approach the recruiters*
   - Find out which agencies recruit in your field and introduce yourself.
   - Don't put yourself up for a job just for the experience, you waste everyone's time including your own. Your lack of commitment will always show through.

10. *Know the rules*
    In any organisation there is always a system. It may be a bit cumbersome, it may be laughable, it may not even work. Learn to work inside it, straight through it or outside it altogether.

Is climbing the corporate ladder a game? Absolutely... If you care about your career you should take these games seriously... If you're an employee you must figure out a way to let the true decision makers know how good you really are, without making enemies of the people in between. Keep your peers as friends... your peers are your natural allies.

M H McCormack,
What They Don't Teach You at Harvard Business School

a word of warning

Whatever the job, being successful requires more than just doing it well. A careful marketing campaign is required to ensure you and your job get the attention they deserve. If you want to get on professionally there is usually a price to pay. You need a strategic plan to make yourself visible. You don't have to pull a series of publicity stunts but you do need to take advantage of any opportunities to highlight your work.

Be careful about the use of heavy advertising. Overt displays of attention-seeking are perceived as pushy or gauche. Superior results are gained by letting your achievements spread by word of mouth. Being associated with a successful project allows other people to say how good you are. It is more subtle and more effective to get to know the influencers professionally than to accost them at a social level.

At the final selection you will not make the team unless you have two key qualities: a sense of humour – the ability to laugh at yourself and to defuse a sensitive situation, and a generous nature – meanness of spirit and pocket in the name of efficiency doesn't open the right doors.

how to avoid a decline

When you've worked hard to achieve the level of visibility you want, how do you avoid becoming an unknown again? The team of authors who put together *High Visibility* – Rein, Kotler and Stoller – aimed their advice at aspiring show-biz entrepreneurs. Their seven obstacles to continued success are valid in any profession or business:

1. Uncontrollable ego – self assurance can grow into arrogance. 'The man is a legend in his own mind.'
2. Unplanned obsolescence – changes outside your control.
3. Uncoupling – leaving a partner, association, group and so losing status.
4. Age – the need to make way for youth.
5. Poor or inconsistent performance.
6. Self-destruction – you do the one thing guaranteed to topple you.
7. Scandal – whether it's true or false, scandal has the capacity to damage or destroy any career.

build your personal brand by projecting a professional image

How you look goes a long way to establishing your identity. What you wear says much about your character and credibility.

Sales and Marketing Management,
August 2000

your professional image: a bridge or a barrier?

Communication style through professional dress can be a bridge or a barrier to clients and customers. 'If they don't like the messenger, they won't get the message.' In a radio interview I heard a senior doctor advocating communication skills training for doctors. She was expressing concern at the poor image of the medical profession. It is true that the awe in which doctors used to be held is being eroded for three reasons:

1. Their inability to apologise for their mistakes because of fear of litigation.
2. Their bedside manner – interpersonal or communication skills, which in many cases are appalling. The high-tech environment of a modern hospital is as much to blame for this as the pressure of a GP's surgery. The result in both cases is that people are seen as a problem that needs treatment, not as people with a problem.
3. The role models of arrogant and distant consultants who are consistently rude to patients and junior staff.

Doctors as well as other professionals need the three As to communicate their professionalism and to be:

Approachable
Accountable
Accessible

If you deal with people as part of your job you need people skills just as much as your professional or technical skills. Your technical skills are taken for granted when someone consults you for the first time. What they are going to 'buy' is you.

Whatever the ingredients of a professional image there are bound to be certain constraints arising from the physical needs of the job, the day-to-day pressures and the expectations and perceptions of that job. What does a personnel manager look like? How should a senior registrar behave? When I asked a mixed group of managers to define 'professionalism' they came up with a surprisingly uniform list of essential qualities:

■ properly qualified;
■ well-informed;
■ discreet;
■ does not allow personal feelings to intrude;
■ does not allow personal prejudice to intrude;
■ does not criticise staff or colleagues in public;

- ▓ does not rubbish a fellow professional;
- ▓ polite;
- ▓ punctual;
- ▓ well prepared;
- ▓ self-disciplined;
- ▓ has a clear belief system;
- ▓ presents an appropriate appearance;
- ▓ does not trade on the insecurities of clients;
- ▓ does not offer professional advice they are not qualified to give;
- ▓ uses a positive approach, does not use sarcasm, or techniques that are humiliating or destructive;
- ▓ practises what they preach;
- ▓ respects confidentiality;
- ▓ respects client reluctance to participate or respond fully (because of social, cultural, financial or emotional constraints).

exercise

Read through the list and consider how these qualities apply to you in your occupation. Do you want to add anything, delete anything or argue?

professional impact

Your professional image is a picture that advertises what you have on offer – a 'promise of delivery'. For most professionals their professional impact boils down to five key qualities: competence, credibility, control, confidence and consistency.

competence

Your competence is the range of abilities that defines what you are able to do – all your skills, talents, qualifications and

Professional impact is made up of six key personal qualities. These are the six 'C's by which we measure each other in business:

Competence

Credibility

Control

Confidence

Consistency

Charisma

experience as well as the things you know you could do but haven't had the opportunity to show just yet. In this context it is useful to analyse:

What you excel at.
What you are good at.
What you can get by on.

You should be majoring, professionally speaking, on what you excel at.

credibility

Your credibility rests on:

■ Looking as though you can do the job and inspiring the belief in others that you can do what you say you can do.

■ Sounding as though you can do the job and inspiring the belief in others that you can deliver what you say you can by using the appropriate language. Do you use the language and technical terms of your specialism correctly? Do you use it to inform rather than baffle, bore or bewilder?

■ Knowing the culture and working within it. It also means knowing the rules, knowing when to abide by them and when you can break them.

control

self-control
Self-control is a mark of maturity. Bad manners and bad temper are equated with lack of control. They show lack of respect to others. Letting your hair down or letting off steam might feel good at the time but could jeopardise the impression you want to create. Check the effect by asking afterwards, 'Was it worth it?'

control of emotion – temper and tears
Sometimes the emotion attached to one activity, event or person spills over on to another. Frustration at a lost contract or difficult case can spill over into unnecessarily sharp words to the next person who phones. Result – temporary loss of reputation. If you give in to emotion at work you lose control and by association you lose competence and credibility. Display anger and you lose the confidence of others as well as revealing a lack of self-confidence. After a bit of a shouting match you might be advised to, 'Take a walk round and cool off.' The hidden message could be, 'Can't risk a display like that in front of our new client. Better take him off this one.' Managed anger in the right circumstances is effective and memorable.

Other outward signs of professional control are:

- ▨ the ability to control others;
- ▨ the ability to control projects, being responsible about resourcing and budgets;
- ▨ the ability to be well-organised and to take control of one's own affairs by dealing efficiently with paperwork and being an effective time-manager.

confidence

Confidence comes from the inside and shows on the outside. There are physiological signs of confidence like standing up straight and breathing easily. There are psychological ones that come from a positive mental attitude and the knowledge that you are well-informed and well-prepared.

Confidence is projected through a vocabulary that uses positive not negative terms and by not under-selling or over-selling your capabilities. Associating with positive and powerful people who value you can reinforce your belief in yourself and recharge your confidence.

consistency

A professional demeanour cannot be put on and taken off like a coat or jacket. Your personal brand has to be consistent to be effective. Your image matters on a daily basis, not just to you but to everyone you meet. The way you look is going to influence how people respond to you, your needs and requests. A favourable impression will work for you well into the future even if it is not needed at the time, so the effort is never wasted. Always be well-dressed and well-presented.

charisma, the gift of grace

Star quality, self-assurance, an air, an aura, charm, confidence – someone with charisma or personal magnetism has a mysterious appeal. Is this quality fixed at birth? Can you learn how to get hold of it? We all know people who walk into a room and fill it with their personality. They command attention and when they speak we are prepared to listen. The way they stand, the way they move and the way they look at you all convey a strong sense of self. If there is a secret it is this last: being charismatic is being strong about who you are on the inside while making space for other people on the outside. Anyone can learn to do more of that.

image stealers

Thieves and robbers abound who will steal from your image and diminish your professional impact. Some robbers are the ones who visit you every day and are even invited by you. Some are encouraged by others and you might not always recognise them when you see them. Here are some you may recognise.

competence robbers

- Self or others can make you seem less capable.
- Not acknowledging your special qualities or the effect of your input, 'It was nothing – anyone could have done it'.
- Being wrong or inaccurate when it really matters.

credibility robbers

- Not knowing what you ought to have known, 'I haven't had time to read the report yet'.

▧ As soon as you insert 'but' you take away the credibility of what you say after it – '...it probably isn't very important but... '.

▧ 'I'm sorry' is a common vocal mannerism and used inappropriately suggests that you are guilty of something and robs you of your previous credibility. Saying sorry too often gives out messages of low self-esteem and low status. If something really was your fault, say 'I apologise – what can I do to put it right?'

▧ Fluffing or flannelling in reply to tricky questions.

control robbers

▧ Being late.
▧ Being disorganised.
▧ Being bad-tempered.
▧ Being bad-mannered.

confidence robbers

▧ A small failure makes you think you are incapable.
▧ A criticism of a particular error or piece of behaviour downgrades your performance in your own mind. 'It was only an idea, I knew it probably wouldn't work... '
▧ Hesitancy in speech.

consistency robbers

▧ Can't be bothered today.
▧ No one will notice.
▧ Having an off-day.

image breakers

There's no accounting for taste, as they say. However, if you are not sure about what might subtract from your professional image, these are examples of what is definitely not on. It applies equally to men and women:

- ■ suede or leather trousers;
- ■ trainers with a suit;
- ■ no bra;
- ■ trousers heavily creased at the crutch;
- ■ cropped top;
- ■ row of pens in top pocket;
- ■ no tights;
- ■ hair ornaments;
- ■ low slung trousers;
- ■ T-shirt with slogan;
- ■ bare leg visible above sock;
- ■ toupee.

the power of grooming

Senior managers, head hunters, managing directors and other people responsible for talent spotting agree that image breakers can be grouped into dress style, clothes maintenance, personal habits and grooming. These are the most common turn-offs:

careless shave	in need of a hair cut
dandruff on collar	chipped nail varnish
overpowering fragrance	poor complexion
strange body odour	unpolished shoes
shoe heels in need of repair	bad breath

I remember a woman who came to see me some years ago as part of a company executive coaching programme. She was being consistently short-listed for internal promotion, interviewed but not selected. She had prepared a good CV and had an excellent track record. The feedback from her latest interview indicated that her personal presentation wasn't quite right. I suggested she brought her prepared interview presentation to our next session and wear her 'interview outfit' for me to look at. She had made an effort but still looked a mess. She had a grasp of the rules but couldn't do it for real. Her dark grey suit and white blouse were of conventionally conservative style for a formal interview but the problem was really one of grooming. Her hair was quite short, wispy, badly cut, no shine. She wore no make up and looked grey and tired. Her hands were rough, nails short and cleanish but with ragged cuticles. She wore flesh-coloured tights that were snagged from knee to ankle and navy shoes that had never seen a coat of polish with heels permanently scuffed from driving. A worn out, large, leather-look shoulder bag over-flowing with junk completed the outfit. She looked like a loser.

Her excuses for her appearance included:

- being too busy with two small children to think about herself;
- being worried that she would appear vain if she spent too much time on her appearance;
- her early childhood conditioning – her parents would have preferred a boy.

Because of her busy lifestyle she had developed bad habits in terms of safeguarding time for looking after herself. She perceived herself to be in a backstage role, rarely seen by anyone 'important'. We did some work on planning an improved lifestyle and from that she was able to raise her self-esteem. She also sharpened her perceptions about the need for a more sophisticated, well-organised, successful image. She began to understand that looking confident, well-dressed and in control would not be misinterpreted as an over-concern with self.

Some people have never developed a routine at all as a result of squalid student days or lack of parental role models. They have a hit and miss system that more or less keeps them clean, respectable and on the road. You need to design a plan that will work for you every day so that you can just forget about it.

business grooming strategy

All over. Stating the obvious, good grooming starts with caring about being clean. There are no exceptions to the rule about starting the day with a shower, bath or wash.

Deodorant. Everyone perspires to a certain degree and it's when perspiration settles on your clothes and you give them a second wearing that the bacteria combine with the air and you get an unpleasant smell. Talcum powder and an effective underarm deodorant are essentials, as is foot spray if you tend to have problem feet. Deodorant removes odour, it doesn't prevent perspiration. If you perspire heavily you will need an anti-perspirant to inhibit perspiration. It is not unhealthy to use an anti-perspirant because sweat will find another way to exit the body.

Hair. For both women and men, hair is an accessory that is worn all the time, so time and money will have to be invested to make sure it sends out appropriate messages all the time. Three vital aspects of hair at any age or stage are: cut, colour and condition. You can see to condition yourself but cut and colour should be dealt with by a professional. A good hairstyle will:

- ■ suit your face shape and colouring;
- ■ suit the texture and thickness of your hair;
- ■ suit your height, body shape and age;
- ■ be appropriate for your life-style.

If hair is long it should not be worn hanging over the face and shoulders or in a complicated style that might collapse.

Women's hair. Most women would rather go to the dentist than the hairdresser. Hair is so important to personal image and self-esteem that it pays to find the right person and put your trust in them. When your hair is cut in a strong shape it is more stylish and presents a positive image. Growing out a perm or an old style is as visually disturbing to other people as it is to you. Make an attempt to control it during the awkward stage.

Men's hair. Most heads of hair grow at a rate of half an inch every two months, so you need regular trims. If you have a bald patch, keep your hair short and avoid bringing longer hair over the bald area to try to conceal it. It has the opposite effect and always looks peculiar.

Men's face. Thorough cleansing followed by a good close shave, then something to soothe and protect the skin.

Men's facial hair. A clean-shaven look is most widely acceptable for a businessman but a beard or moustache are often worn in the more creative or academic fields. If you sport a beard you run the risk of losing credibility in the more conservative occupations such as accountancy, insurance and sales. Your beard should reflect your personality and be a part of you. A beard is not an easy option, it requires a great deal of maintenance in the form of trimming and shampooing. The surrounding facial area needs regular shaving and moisturising as well. A moustache can be a strong style statement. It can also look silly. Try to take an objective look at yours. Hair in nose and ears: your barber should be able to clip it if you can't see to it yourself. Eyebrows that meet over the bridge of the nose look a bit Neanderthal rather than virile.

Women's face. Start with the cleanse–tone–moisturise routine even if you wear little or no make-up. Skilfully applied cosmetics with a light touch give a polish to your business image. If you use foundation, check hair line and jawline for a smooth finish and that the colour blends with your natural skin tone. Check your collar for marks. If you are not sure how to use cosmetics effectively or feel you need an update, visit a professional make-up artist for a lesson.

Women's facial hair. An obvious moustache or a bristly chin are a bit disconcerting in a culture that does not find facial hair attractive.

Your face. Do you have a skin fitness programme? Is your complexion healthy and spot-free or does it look greying and uncared for? Business professionals, like everyone else, are exposed to the aggressive conditions of modern living which take their toll on the skin. Signs of 'added' ageing occur alongside natural ageing and are caused not only by the stress of travelling and pollution but also by exposure to sun, wind, cold and smoky atmospheres.

Shoulders. Check for dandruff, dust and loose hairs. Brush well before leaving base. Keep a clothes brush at work or in your briefcase.

Teeth. In good condition, well brushed, no traces of breakfast or lipstick. If you have neglected your teeth because of a fear of the dentist, or unhappy childhood experiences, check that this aspect of your appearance is not proving to be a multiple liability. People who are self-conscious about bad teeth rarely smile, and cover their mouth with their hands when they laugh or speak. This mannerism could be perceived as lack of confidence or shiftiness. Use sugar-free mints or a breath freshening spray after drinks or food if meeting clients or customers.

Hands and nails. Should be clean without evidence of DIY, gardening or decorating. Nails should be clean, not too long, with an unobtrusive manicure.

Fragrance. Not everyone enjoys the same smells. For an important meeting, leave it off, don't risk offending before you have even opened your mouth. If you do wear a fragrance choose a light or floral one that is not too heavy or spicy. Make sure that after-shave and perfume don't get onto your clothes. The alcohol content and the colouring could cause staining. Stale fragrance smells just that – stale.

> Whatever personal fashion style a woman has evolved for herself, it will always be doubly reinforced by the best of grooming.
>
> Toni Williams, image consultant

who makes the rules?

Most people would agree that what you wear to work does matter. *But* – how do you decide what is appropriate and to whom do you listen? There is an increasing feeling that it shouldn't matter what you wear – that somehow to dictate or even suggest what you should wear is an infringement of personal liberty. Different occupations and different bosses set the tone for different kinds of work 'uniforms'. A decision about what to wear to work or for a special situation such as a presentation or an interview will be influenced by personal needs and the expectations of the 'audience'. It will be subtly influenced by social and economic trends.

Your choice will have to take into account what the dress code of the organisation will support. In some organisations the dress code is written down in a staff handbook and rigidly adhered to. In others there are rules that are unwritten and unspoken and operate by example. In many companies where I have worked as a consultant, a conservatively-styled dark suit and light shirt are the only option for senior women and men.

You have to make the decision – how do you decide what image to project? Whatever the circumstances your decision will be based on:

- ▓ the expectations of your audience;
- ▓ the prevailing culture;
- ▓ the perceptions surrounding your occupation;
- ▓ where you work, its geographical location;
- ▓ the nature of the job, what you actually do all day, the physical aspects;
- ▓ what kind of image you need to project;
- ▓ your personal style, personality, temperament, goals and values and level of ambition.

default business outfit

Be ready for emergencies. When in doubt, always have the default outfit ready. This means that, even at the start of the 21st century, in order to look professional you need to wear a suit because a suit always looks right. If you are under 35 you may never have owned a suit, so aim for the New Traditionalist look, a relaxed suit that combines a subtle texture with a flattering colour – much more modern than a stiff, over-fitted suit in a dark, dull colour worn with a white shirt.

You need it when you want a 'safe' business outfit that will see you through your daily life and most business situations if you have no clue about what to wear. If you have an interview, press call or business presentation, you will find it really useful to have the default outfit clean and ready to wear at a moment's notice, even if it is not your usual get-up.

The suit is perfect for when times are hard, because it effortlessly projects seriousness, respect and self-discipline. A suit saves time because all the bits work together without effort on the wearer's part.

default business outfit for men

the suit option

At the time of writing, the single-breasted suit with strong shoulder line and slim cut is still a fashion basic for men and should flatter most body types. This jacket style looks best worn with flat front or single pleat trousers. Double-breasted suits have gone in and out of fashion over the last decade but are beginning to be seen again, so if a double breasted style is most flattering to you, then look for the new cut with four or six buttons.

- **Suit:** a comfortable, well fitting suit in a conservative but not stuffy style, in a medium to dark tone of navy or grey is considered businesslike and respectable.
- **Shirt:** a lighter colour shirt – off-white, cream, pink, pale blue, soft grey, lavender – looks businesslike. Also use stronger colours while they are still fashionable and if you like them.
- **Tie:** even if you are not a tie wearer, collect several ties that can form part of your default outfit. Choose ties with a discreet pattern in which blue or red predominates, not flowery, not funny, not loud. A tie like this will work with all the above shirt colours. Also a deeper shade toned within lighter shades of the same colour family is always safe: burgundy always works with pink, navy always works with pale blue, charcoal grey always works with soft grey and purple always works with lavender.
- **Shoes:** black, polished, in good repair, check laces for fraying. No trainers, sandals or boots – remember this is the 'safe' outfit.
- **Socks:** black is the only colour to wear with black shoes really and is always a stylish as well as safe option. Have two pairs ready in case of an emergency.

- **Accessories:** stick to plain silver or gold for cufflinks and belt buckles, no other jewellery, laptop (plus any of its important accessories) in a neat case, briefcase, good quality pen and notebook or organiser, your business cards.

The greatest thing about a suit is that it makes you feel sharp and ready for work. It's a one-stop instant fix of all the elements you need – businesslike, stylish and easy to deal with.

Dylan Jones, Editor, *GQ*

tip

If the shirt has double cuffs and a stiffened collar, keep a pair of cufflinks ready in the buttonholes and insert the collar stiffeners as soon as the shirt has been ironed, in case you forget on the day.

the jacket option
You can use the same plan as above but substitute a jacket and trousers for a suit in more informal environments.

default business outfit for women

the suit option
Suits are back. They have never really gone away. A suit is anonymous, a safe option, and sends out a message of professionalism without you having to try too hard.

- **Suit:** a comfortable, well fitting skirt or trouser suit in a conservative but not stuffy style. Medium to dark neutrals are the safest choice; navy, beige, taupe or grey are considered to be businesslike and respectable. If you prefer brighter colours then something flattering like soft red, rust, pine green or soft blue would work; or you could go for an interesting surface texture such as silk tweed, herringbone weave or chenille according to your taste and personal colouring.

■ **Shoes:** black, polished, in good repair. Court shoes (cut low on the top of the foot) with a skirt, trouser shoes (cut high on the top of the foot) with trousers. Not trainers, sandals or boots: remember this is the 'safe' outfit.

■ **Hosiery:** if in doubt, 10 denier 'barely black' always work. Keep two pairs available, one to wear and one to take with you in case of accidents.

■ **Accessories:** jewellery, stick to the real thing, for example gold, silver or pearls; not cheap ethnic pieces or diamonds. A couple of silk or velvet scarves are useful (one long and narrow, one square); a handbag that goes with everything; laptop (plus any of its important accessories) in a neat case; briefcase; good quality pen and notebook or organiser; your business cards.

the jacket option

If you do not like wearing suits or feel they are too formal for most of the situations you will find yourself in, then the jacket option could work for you. For this option the money goes on the best jacket you can afford. Think in terms of three units: top plus middle plus bottom.

■ **Top:** one great jacket will do the job here, but you might find it useful to have two or more jackets in different styles (eg collarless, zip front, with revers) in either medium or dark neutrals (or according to your taste and personal colouring you could use a flattering colour such as soft red, rust, pine green or soft blue, or a definite surface texture such as silk tweed, herringbone weave or chenille). The effect is achieved with the jacket, so keep the middle and bottom colours coordinated and simple.

- ■ **Middle:** blouse, shirt, tee-shirt in white, cream, grey, navy or black.
- ■ **Bottom:** trousers or skirt to match or contrast with the top or middle in beige, cream, grey, navy or black depending on the season.
- ■ Shoes and hosiery as above.

The jacket option gives you the opportunity to create a variety of looks from a bare minimum of items.

the dress and jacket option

Jackets can also be worn over a plain dress that either matches or coordinates with the jacket. A matching dress and jacket in a dark neutral is the most formal.

tip

Have a skirt or trousers that matches or nearly matches your darkest, most sober jacket, so that you can turn your outfit into a 'nearly suit' if the occasion is more formal than you realised.

tip

Spend some money. Focus on quality not quantity. If an expensive suit is not a realistic option for you, then buy some good shirts and take your jacket off when at work. Cheap suits spell failure.

dressing down

Only workers who never come face to face with customers or senior managers can still fearlessly wear jeans and T-shirts – with the notable exception of technical staff, of whom nothing smarter was ever expected in the first place.

business casual: some thoughts from the field

The backlash against suits revealed a labour market so tight that workers had all the cards. Bosses hated seeing their staff slouch contemptuously in torn jeans and jumpers, but had to put up with it. Now, jobs are harder to come by, and involve more work and less play. The suit is back. Everywhere except the *Economist*, of course. Here freedom of movement is religion.

Economist, February 2001

Life at work, including what to wear, has got more complicated and confusing. What did work well for us was Dress Down Friday as a celebration that the weekend was almost here. I don't think the British male has found the right half-way uniform between traditional business dress and scruffy that is not the 'blazer from the golf club' – we don't seem to be able to get that Italian look.

Roger Miles, Partner in Deloitte and Touche

Our dress code is smart business dress, we do not insist on suits but strictly no jeans or trainers. A lot of staff do wear suits as they like to look professional and tend to get more respect from clients.

Polly Sampson

I would welcome a return to more formal business attire for all people who work in offices. The relaxed dress code of the last few years has done little to promote a professional image and has led to much confusion about 'what to wear'. This has resulted in people dressing in any kind of outfit from a tailored suit to jeans with an open-neck shirt.

Patricia Day, Assistant Secretary, BT Group

How smart are we as a nation, I wonder? We don't do casual dressing well mainly because we're the wrong shape, we don't have that Continental elegance, we're just not chic. Because of this inherent disadvantage we have to adhere to basic rules. For example, if we're visiting a West End law firm, it's not a question of is it a suit, but is it a grey or black suit? Anything rash in the way of colour is restricted to the blouse or tie.

If it was a local government client then, like many of the more informal organisations, they don't make judgements about appearance because it's not culturally acceptable.

Jennifer Bowden, Managing Consultant, Human Resource Solutions

The thing is everybody wants to look busy and if you don't have a suit on, you obviously don't have a client meeting to go to – people will take note of that.

Report on Lehman Bros return to traditional city dress, *The Times*, January 2002

In early 2002 Lehman Brothers, the US investment bank, signalled a return to traditional City dress, supporting the theory that the 'preppy' look (of which it was an early champion) had outlived its popularity. The debate covers the perceived advantages and disadvantages of business casual:

For	Against
■ Breaks down hierarchical barriers	■ More flirtatious behaviour (danger of litigation)
■ Cheaper to buy	■ Increase in sexist jokes
■ Lower maintenance costs	■ Increase in absenteeism
■ Boosts morale	■ Fosters environment ripe for sexual harassment
■ More creative environment	■ Induces slacking off
■ More comfortable to wear	■ Encourages a laissez fair attitude
■ Increases productivity	

build your personal brand by packaging your personality

> Once you are past the basic warmth and decency requirement, buying clothes is as much about how they fit your head as how they look on your body.
>
> Brenda Polan, *Evening Standard*, 2001

clothes and personality

How do you come across? Your early social conditioning, your background, experience of life, your education and genetic inheritance all contribute to your view of yourself and to your attitude to the world. These internal elements are externalised through:

- The way you behave with other people
- The image you project
- The values you hold
- The kind of language and vocabulary you use
- Your communication style
- Your total impact, the sum of all of the parts that triggers a response from others

A successful dresser finds a distinctive way of dressing that is appropriate for what they do and is a true reflection of their personality. Once developed it can be adapted for any occasion. This sounds simple but is not so easy to do. Many people find it difficult even to begin to think about it.

Not everyone thinks about clothes in the same way. The way they've been brought up, their self-esteem, their self-image and their personality will all influence how they arrive at decisions when they shop for clothes and when they get dressed. Some people avoid the process altogether and wear a uniform every day. Some, especially but not exclusively men, allow themselves to be dressed by others – their wives, mothers, friends or shop assistants.

Imagine that there are two polar opposites of preference to do with how you think and feel about clothes. At one end is the person who loves clothes and uses clothes to express moods and feelings, the 'expressive' dresser, and at the opposite end is the negative or 'functional' dresser who only wears clothes to keep warm and modest. Where would you position yourself on the 'Clothes Line'?

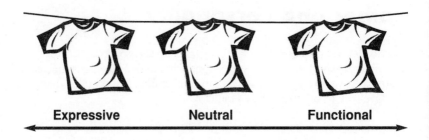

| Expressive | Neutral | Functional |

assessing clothing personality

Even if they find it a bit difficult to think objectively about clothing, people can usually position themselves accurately on the 'Clothes-line' – an imaginary line of thinking and feeling about clothes which runs from *Neutral* out to the extremes of *Expressive* and *Functional*. Finding out where you position yourself is a useful tool to aid future decisions about business dress.

The neutral dresser has an unfocused sense of self, dresses to a 'recipe' often learnt in youth or early childhood, perhaps at boarding school, armed forces or from a protective and unimaginative mother. They can be wary of seeming vain if they pay too much attention to appearance. Though their grooming may be acceptable there is a lack of style awareness and 'street cred'. Their level of awareness of what others may deduce from their appearance is also low. They know they have to get dressed because society expects it but they neither relish nor dread the activity – it is merely routine. Their dress style is recognisable from its conformity, uninspired co-ordination and budget consciousness.

Expressive dressers enjoy clothes. They enjoy getting dressed and selecting what to wear. They always make an effort regardless of time, place or occasion and would do so whether or not they had an audience. Attention to detail is important to them and they take trouble to co-ordinate their outfits and are always well-groomed. Recognisable by their celebratory attitude to dressing, their clothes fit well and are well-maintained. They use clothes as an expression of personality and feeling. They have a positive self-image and their behaviour can tip over into obsession with clothes and appearance. Because the way they dress is an expression of individuality, the expressive would be horrified to meet someone dressed in exactly the same outfit. Expressive dressers can also use clothes as a hiding place, to act a part or as an outward manifestation of inner conflict or struggle.

Functional dressers dislike having to bother about clothes. They can look scruffy and uncoordinated. Their clothes are not well maintained, clean or pressed and do not fit well. Negativity can arise from either high or low self-esteem or a superior attitude. 'People will have to take me as I am'. Or it can come from a strong inner sense of self with no need to acknowledge external factors.

Some people make themselves deliberately unattractive out of anger. The way they look is a tangible expression of how they feel. Their anger may be at being overweight, young, disabled or different. They feel short-changed. The more unattractive they make themselves the more they suffer. The teenage girl who hides behind a curtain of long hair, wearing a long shapeless cardigan with the sleeves drooping down past her fingertips, is masking her anger and confusion about her developing maturity.

something for the neutral dresser

It is interesting that, although British fashion designers are renowned for their creativity and flair... few are producing the sort of professional, elegant garments British women so desperately need. A quick flick through the fashion magazines reveals wild flights of fancy: see-through and sexy ensembles, photographed in weird locations, and worn by strange looking 16 year olds.

Alice Rawsthorn, *FT*'s design and architecture critic, writing in *Management Today*

advice from a celebratory dresser

If you're not going to dress as though your life depends on it – don't bother to get out of bed!

Leigh Bowery, one of Brighton's famous cross-dressers, performance artist and clubber

message for a functional dresser

And the prophet answered:

Your clothes conceal much of your beauty, yet they hide not the unbeautiful.

And though you seek in garments the freedom of privacy you may find in them a harness and a chain.

Kahlil Gibran, *The Prophet*

clothes snobs

Some people set up conscious or unconscious barriers that prevent them from dressing appropriately. I meet many mani-festations of the clothing personality types I have described. Some of them are snobs. They are convinced that their style and their attitude are superior to everyone else's. Clothes snobs come in many sub-types. Here are some of them:

The 'fashion' snob. Takes an intellectually superior stance to fashion and clothing and presents a consistently dowdy appear-ance. They have a low understanding of the power of appear-ance and self-image. They see dress-sense as a superficial concern. Sometimes naive or unwordly, they make unconscious sartorial errors – running shoes with shirt and tie, court shoes with jogging bottoms, inexpertly matched colours, textures and patterns. They cannot conceive of a 'total look'. Clothes are grouped according to function not image.

The 'personality' snob. The kind of person who thinks they have so much personal charisma that they can wear what they like. They have such confidence in their own style that they don't welcome advice from anyone, particularly image consul-tants. Only they know how to dress themselves because they know themselves so well. The result is that they often present an image that is slightly quaint. The 'personality' snob is fond of visual 'jokes'. They can often dress well for a special occa-sion like a dinner and dance or a fancy dress party. They pride themselves on knowing the right thing to wear if necessary – but the decision is dictated by them not the situation.

The 'quality' snob. Will only wear 'good' clothes and can't understand that beauty, style, originality or flair can come from any other source. They will be well-dressed but usually just miss being stylish from fear of appearing vulgar or cheap. They are unwilling to take risks with quality for the sake of style, comfort or fashion. They are highly label-conscious and gain their security from status labels. They can be classic or fashion dressers. 'If it's a Gucci it must be OK!' Not always *nouveau riche*, typically they feel insecure about their own taste and style. A measure of their insecurity is the label worn on the outside. The quality snob tag also applies to the *nouveau pauvre* who have always dressed from Aquascutum and Burberry even if their clothes are now in shreds.

The 'social' snob. Doesn't mind being dressed in a similar fashion to others round them, in fact they derive a certain security from this. Social dressers want to dress in the same outfit and will order (from a catalogue or a couturier depending on their status) a similar garment to a friend or colleague. Whether it be at Ascot or for a rave, peer group solidarity is demonstrated when individuals wear a similar range of garments to appear at the same social event. Social dressers are conformist dressers. They consider what other people will or might be wearing before they make their decision. When they all look the same, they are then convinced of the rightness of their decision. They fail to see why anyone would want to look different.

The 'avant-garde' snob. This kind of dresser wears clothing in styles that have not yet reached the general consumer. As soon as the look hits the high street or preferably before then, they have moved on to something else. This kind of dresser needs an audience, preferably of the same type as themselves who will understand the nuances of their interpretations. They can be fashion victims but can also be creative and original dressers and keen watchers of trends. They mock conservatism.

self-expression v. function

People who are unable to express themselves through the way they dress for their job feel unbearably restricted and usually opt for an unsuitable compromise. Others have developed a style that suits them off-duty but is hopelessly inappropriate for their professional life. Some people I know have managed to integrate their dress style with their lifestyle in a very successful way.

> I never have any difficulty deciding what to wear, I like clothes but don't really follow fashion. I know what suits me and have a 'costume' for every occasion.
>
> Alan Felton, actor and theatrical historian

The 'political' dresser. Use their clothes to make a statement socially and professionally. By their own standards, they have to be the best-dressed person at any event. They don't mind being looked at – in fact their style is wasted without an audience. Their clothes can inform, entertain, amuse or revoke but they won't be ignored. They don't always understand that the expression of their view, verbally or non-verbally, is not the most important thing on the agenda.

The 'economic' dresser. Can't bring themselves to buy any item of clothing unless it's a bargain. They haunt sales and factory shops. Spending as little as possible is more important to them than the style, colour or suitability of a garment. They often have a wardrobe full of mistakes which are actually costing them a fortune because they are never worn. They can be shrewd shoppers but often sacrifice quality for price. They may feel guilty about spending money on themselves and when they buy for themselves assuage their guilt by buying a present for someone else as well – usually the children. Women do this more often than men. They don't see that dressing cheaply will be perceived as a lack of self-esteem. Occasionally they sport a winner – more by luck than judgement – and look stunning.

The 'body-conscious' dresser. Often well-proportioned with good body tone. This may be either by accident or design, but typically a body-conscious dresser will watch their weight, work out or play sport. They like to display what they perceive to be their assets in tight-fitting clothing, low fronts, undoing strategic buttons, pushing sleeves up to display a tan. Belts, lycra, bright colours and immaculate grooming are their hall-marks. They don't always see that too obvious a display of sexuality harms their professional image.

'Dramatic' dressers. Play a part and have a costume for everything. They are often striking-looking themselves and dress to match. Whether they are playing the part of stock-broker, weekend sailor, holidaymaker, caring professional or sparkling hostess, they've got all the gear. They are amazed that not everyone wants to dress up. They can be glamorous and stylish and push the elements of their look to extremes. They don't realize that they can look over-dressed, hard or intimidating.

The 'comfort' dresser. The first rule of clothing choice for this person is that all garments must be physically comfortable. They require clothes to fit without pinching or itching. They won't wear anything that is too tight or droopy, or that needs constant fixing. They presume that smart clothes will be uncomfortable. They often use their expressed need for comfort to disguise laziness or not being able to cope with a more sophisticated style of dress and look about as elegant as a bag of groceries.

colour and personality
why navy is an ideal colour for business

Because it is a combination of blue and black. Blue has the ability to create calm and symbolises dignity and truth (it is no accident that so many financial institutions, banks and insurance companies incorporate medium-blue tones into their corporate logo). Black adds weight and power, both symbolically and visually. Unrelieved black (although dramatic and sophisticated in different environments) is too intense for professional dressing; dark brown is too sad; light grey is too insubstantial.

the problem with pink for business

Psychologically, pink has been judged 'the sweetest colour' because according to research findings (by Vargas, in 1986), pink causes the hypothalamus to signal the adrenal glands to slow their secretions, thus reducing the heart rate and blocking anger.

Human beings are born with a variety of innate responses. One of the most powerful of these is our response to colour. Most of us have strong likes and dislikes with regard to colour. It does not matter why we do; it is just useful to recognise that we have strong responses. There are four ways of considering our response to colour:

- Colour associations: symbolic, cultural, historical, psychological or other associations.
- Personality indications: what your choice of colour reveals about some aspect of your psychology.
- Appropriateness: a colour's perceived suitability for use in a professional wardrobe.
- Aesthetics: how colours can flatter the wearer and the rules for pleasing colour combinations.

Colour responses, personality indications and appropriateness for use in a professional wardrobe are considered below. The aesthetics are covered in Chapter Five.

black

■ *Associations:* dramatic, elegant, death and mourning, heavy, old, solid.

■ *Personality indications:* sophisticated, lazy, everyone else wears it, doesn't show the dirt, going through a time of indecision, choices to be made.

■ *Suitability for professional dressing:* not head to foot but fine as top, middle or bottom garments or as accessories. A daunting colour if you work with children or the elderly. Black shows up ironing marks, dust, fluff and cat's hair.

white (including soft whites, ivory and cream)

■ *Associations:* cleanliness, purity, hospitals, hygiene, sterility, winter, peace.

■ *Personality indications:* can be neutral, a non-communicator, over-fussy, concerned with order and cleanliness.

■ *Suitability for professional dressing:* good for shirts and blouses, not suitable head to foot, not accessories. Could use for high impact image at a conference or sales presentation. Avoid if you don't enjoy spending time, effort or money on grooming and laundering.

grey

■ *Associations:* neutral, ethereal, artistic, respectability, modesty, old age.

■ *Personality indications:* reliable, balanced, conservative, unwilling to make commitments, unwilling to make themselves visible.

■ *Suitability for professional dressing:* excellent through all tones, but needs a small injection of colour to make it interesting. Not suitable for accessories except as a fashion statement by a woman. Less authoritarian than black and dark navy. Suitable when negotiating a contract or dispute. Good for interviews when worn with white or a flattering colour. Grey does not make an impact in the creative arena unless the cut is non-traditional.

magenta

■ *Associations:* considered to be an 'artificial' colour, feminine, glamorous (sometimes called 'tart's pink'!).
■ *Personality indications:* rather a dramatic personal style, likes company, likes an audience, can be a bit self-centred, is confident and self-assured.
■ *Suitability for professional dressing:* not top to toe, not for men, not for leather accessories, good for silk. In its softer forms acceptable as men's ties. Is rather unpopular as a presentation colour, projects hard, tough, brittle, lack of sensitivity. Can look elegant on a woman for formal, outdoor events.

soft pinks (including raspberry, coral, candy floss and peach)

■ *Associations:* the colour for girl babies, candy floss, roses.
■ *Personality indications:* approachable, feminine, sentimental – could be a soft touch.
■ *Suitability for professional dressing:* use sparingly to soften harder, darker and neutral colours. Not for leather accessories. Baby pinks do not indicate management material. Good for shirts in the lighter tints.

red

- ■ *Associations:* the colour of hearts and flames, stands for power and sexuality, hot, dangerous, passionate.
- ■ *Personality indications:* passionate, needs to be right, a leader, can be aggressive, a bit overbearing, is willing to take risks, sign of emotional strength, confident, exciting.
- ■ *Suitability for professional dressing:* not head to foot, not for leather accessories. Good for woman's jacket, blouse or scarf, or man's tie. Right for occasions when you need to be recognised. Wrong for when you are tired or depressed and not able to live up to it.

orange (including tangerine, peach and pumpkin)

- ■ *Associations:* warm, Jaffa oranges, energy, hospitality.
- ■ *Personality indications:* likes to have fun, is a sociable type, not always very self-disciplined, a bit common, flighty.
- ■ *Suitability for professional dressing:* only in small quantities. The least professional colour, it can look cheap and immediately downgrades status.

yellow

- ■ *Associations:* the colour of sunshine, daffodils, bananas, cowardice and deceit.
- ■ *Personality indications:* rather disorganised, outgoing, has creative thoughts, sense of humour, impulsive, is willing to experiment. Cheerful, optimistic, lively, happy, a bit juvenile at times.
- ■ *Suitability for professional dressing:* only in small quantities, woman's jacket if cut is conservative.

Yellow has frivolous connotations so is not good for serious business meetings. Yellow/black combination worn by nature's aggressors.

greens (including grass green, olive, moss, pine)

■ *Associations:* tranquil and pastoral, fresh, the colour of trees and grass, associated with fertility and magic but is also the colour of mildew, poison and jealousy.
■ *Personality indications:* a nurturer, prefers informality, helpful, a bit shy, kind, tends to laziness, boring, predictable.
■ *Suitability for professional dressing:* only in small quantities, women's jacket if cut is conservative, men's tie as part of a pattern. The deeper greens are acceptable business wear for women but not for men unless dressing down, or more fashionable dress is the norm.

blue green

■ *Associations:* the sea, tranquillity, repose, informality.
■ *Personality indications:* perfectionist, polite, likes tidiness but not necessarily order, likes family traditions and special occasions.
■ *Suitability for professional dressing:* only in small quantities, women's jacket if cut is conservative, men's tie as part of a pattern. Introduces a note of casualness or informality to darker colours. Popular colour. Doesn't offend people.

blue

■ *Associations:* the colour of the sky and sea, space, calm, depression, the most popular and the most worn colour in the Western world. Medium blues look good on TV. Light blue looks young and sporty.

■ *Personality indications:* calm, friendly, conservative. Slow to trust but loyal when trust is deserved.

■ *Suitability for professional dressing:* light blue in the summer and for shirts and blouses, medium blue for ties, jackets, shirts and trousers. Only the darkest shades suitable for suits. Blue and creativity and originality don't go together so won't be right for PR, design or marketing if pitching an alternative approach or solution.

navy

■ *Associations:* royal, deep and navy blues have associations with esteem, dignity and wealth.

■ *Personality indications:* organised, conservative, logical, neutral. Prefers classic looks and objects. May not respond eagerly to new ideas or new methods.

■ *Suitability for professional dressing:* Excellent, but needs a touch of colour to keep it interesting. Doesn't promote success and confidence to strangers unless worn in classic Establishment style and in good quality.

purple and lavender (from periwinkle to plum)

■ *Associations:* a strong violet is not often found in nature and so is considered an artificial, sometimes vulgar, colour. Purple is dramatic and sophisticated and associated with royalty and dignity, lavender and lilac with Oscar Wilde and poetry and sensitivity.

■ *Personality indications:* artistic, sensitive, intuitive, slow, daydreamer, good listener, spiritual, impractical.

▓ *Suitability for professional dressing:* mid-tone and deep purples are alternatives for women who don't have to wear conservative navies and greys. An alternative to black for glamour. Not suitable for men except in small quantities. Dark and light tones can be very effective mixed in the form of a pattern for a tie or worn as braces.

brown (including chocolate, golden and earthy tones)

▓ *Associations:* rich and fertile like the earth or sad and wistful like damp autumn leaves. Associations with piety as in a monk's habit.

▓ *Personality indications:* close to the earth, dislikes pretensions, solid, natural, needs to look after people, unsophisticated, homely.

▓ *Suitability for professional dressing:* the darker, blacker browns work as an alternative to the more conservative greys and navies for men and women. Good for leather accessories. The richer, warmer browns are unthreatening and will help people to open up to you. At public functions you are likely to disappear into the woodwork.

selecting colours for business dressing

Selecting appropriate colours for business dress will depend on:

▓ The need to send symbolic messages: chairing a trade union meeting, will you need your red tie to show your socialist affiliations?

▓ Utility: are you a natural attractor of dirt? If you are, your choice will be governed by the need for darker, more practical colours so that you look the part and are not let down by maintenance problems.

■ Personal style: colour has the ability to convey strong messages about personal style. We need to have colours that will help us to blend in, as well as to make us memorable.

■ Expectations: the colours that are expected in your role and at your level. You may be limited by convention to light and dark neutrals or your status may allow you to use opportunities to be more creative with colour.

■ Mood: we start the day by being guided by our intuition. The colours we choose can enhance or underplay current mood. If you feel positive and full of beans, wearing red or yellow could exhaust everyone round you by the end of the day. If you are feeling fed up, opt for the more cheerful colours to give you a spiritual lift.

design and personality

Do you consider yourself to be well dressed for work? If you do, you will probably be wearing clothes that obey a certain set of rules. Whatever the occasion you will have selected an outfit that:

■ suits your personality;
■ feels comfortable;
■ is fit for the purpose;
■ is aesthetically pleasing – following the rules of good design.

The basic components of design include colour, line, shape, detail, pattern and texture. These are the tools used to implement the principles of balance, proportion, harmony, emphasis and contrast. This simple set of rules will help you to co-ordinate your business wardrobe.

ten basic design guidelines
colour

Choose a maximum of three colours in any outfit, making sure one is a neutral.

example
Men: grey (neutral) suit plus lilac shirt plus purple tie.

Women: plum jacket plus black (neutral) trousers plus plum and blackcurrant scarf.

line and shape

Select clothes and accessories that have clean, uncluttered lines and simple shapes.

example
Women: avoid wearing garments where two collars overlap; avoid long hair, a scarf and a necklace.

detail

Use fine construction or decorative detail as a focal point, not all over.

example
Men: avoid four button cuffs, with fancy cufflinks and monogrammed cuffs.

pattern

As a general rule, avoid mixing patterns in the same outfit. If you do mix patterns then use contrast in scale.

example

Men: contrast small against medium; wear a tie with a plain background and tiny dots with a shirt in medium stripes.

Women: contrast large against small; wear a scarf in a bold print with a blouse in a tiny check.

texture

Consciously combine textures to create visual interest, for example crunchy with smooth, tight weave with loose weave.

example

Women: a shirt in soft, shiny silk worn with dull wool crepe trousers.

Men: a herringbone weave shirt worn with a silk tie.

balance

Seek to find visual balance by compensating for an element that is too light or too heavy, in colour or tone or silhouette.

example

Men: dark shoes add visual weight and 'ground' a lighter outfit.

Women: some width at shoulder level will balance a pear-shaped figure.

proportion

Do you recall the rule of the Golden Mean: 3:5, 5:8, 8:13? In simple terms we could say that unequal proportions are more dynamic visually. They do not have to be measurably accurate but they should be observable, so you would use two different, not same elements from this simple model:

very short – short – medium – long – very long

example
Women: short with short is boring, short with very short is interesting; long with long is boring, long with medium is more dynamic.

harmony

When putting together an outfit, select garments that connect with each other through a conscious design theme, picking up a common element of colour, style or fashion. Make sure that each garment is 'going to the same party'.

contrast

Contrasting elements make for visual impact and drama. You can aim for contrast in any of the preceding elements.

example
- ▓ light/dark colours;
- ▓ heavy/lightweight fabrics;
- ▓ full shapes/narrow shapes.

emphasis

Emphasise your personality or fashion style by using your 'style signature' in every single outfit

example
Men: hand-made shirts, or always wear cufflinks or coloured lining to jackets.

Women: hand-crafted jewellery, or same colour family for everything, or strong hair style.

O Wad some Power the giftie gi'e us
To see oursels as others see us!
It would frae mony a blunder free us
And foolish notion:
What airs in dress and gait wad lea'e us
And ev'n devotion
Robert Burns (1759–1796), *To a louse – on seeing one on a lady's bonnet at church*

build your personal brand by organising your business wardrobe

The sense of being well-dressed gives a feeling of inward tranquillity which religion is powerless to bestow.

Miss C Forbes (1817–1911)
confiding to her diary

building an appropriate business wardrobe

Coco Chanel believed that above all else, clothes should be logical. Consider the logic of your business wardrobe and clothing needs. Everyone needs a formal business suit in a conservative cut and colour for the most formal aspects of their working life – interviews, presentations and so on. After that it is simply a question of having the right number of garments – tops, middles and bottoms, plus their accessories – so that you have a logical, simple, co-ordinated system that will never let you down.

Before you start organising and planning, collect some important personal data:

- ■ about your immediate visual and physical impact;
- ■ about your own colouring and your colour preferences;
- ■ about your personal architecture, your defining physical characteristics.

Anyone can wear any colour! It just depends on the tone of that colour. The most flattering colours are those that are in harmony with your own natural colouring. You can estimate which colour direction it flows in by looking at the colour of your skin, hair and eyes.

- ■ **Depth** – ranges from deep, dark tones through medium to light.
- ■ **Clarity** – ranges from clear, clean, bright tones through to soft, muted shades.
- ■ **Undertone** – ranges from yellow based (warm) colours through to blue-based (cool) colours.

objective observation

Objective observation is the technique of looking to really see and attempting to see yourself as others see you. It helps people tune into themselves visually. They learn to look without listening so that they can concentrate on the visual messages. Look in the mirror and assess what you see without being judgemental. Avoid the trap of letting self-deception or emotional baggage mist over what is really there. This is not meant to cause a blip in your self-esteem but to stop you either dwelling on the negatives (typically a female response) or being unrealistically positive (the usual male response).

exercise

The first stage of this exercise is like having a scan in hospital. Dress as you would for an ordinary working day. Scan slowly from top to toe, side to side, back and front and just see what's there. Attempt to be dispassionate, as though you were looking at a stranger. The second stage is to make an objective assessment about the assets and liabilities of your appearance – physical characteristics, clothes and grooming. Decide which aspects are positively working for your professional image, project your personality and accurately reflect your personal standards, goals and objectives. Then consider honestly which aspects are liabilities and could be forming a barrier to your success.

image scan

Smile. A genuine smile at the appropriate time and place is a great asset; it's friendly, disarming, confident.

Sparkle in the eyes. Does it show a sense of humour, energy and enthusiasm?

Facial expression. Some people have the kind of face that goes sour or cross-looking or tired when in repose. A frown appears, the mouth moves down and the chin juts out a bit. This look doesn't necessarily mean you are depressed or angry, you just look as though you are. Do people always make comments about your expression and say things like, 'Cheer up', 'What's wrong with you?' If this happens to you, ask for a second opinion. Some people say these things and don't mean them, it's just an irritating mannerism. If you've got one of those faces, however, try raising your eyebrows and widening your eyes occasionally at meetings or during an interview. This will release the frown and bring the corners of the mouth up.

Posture. Do you stand straight and give an air of self-assurance and confidence, or do you stoop or cross your legs and cross your arms in an over-protective manner? Do you think you come across as aggressive, domineering, weak or submissive? Ask someone for a second opinion.

Fitness. Do you look fit and well or a bit tired and stressed? By looking as though you have energy and take care of yourself physically, people will presume you will be able to manage other things just as well. If you are not fit and well – why not? Can you do anything about it? If you can't then you can dress well, have immaculate grooming, think, speak and act positively and shift the focus away from your illness or disability.

Weight. If you are under-weight or over-weight for your height and build and feel self-conscious about it, are you compensating by dressing, standing or sitting in a way that projects your perceived liabilities instead of your assets?

Height. Do you think you are too tall or too small? Check that you are not over-compensating. A woman of five foot two in very high heels simply looks as though she's trying too hard. A man over six foot who stoops is unconsciously apologising for his height and loses status.

Glasses. Do they fit, do they suit you, are they polished, are they up to date? Old-fashioned glasses are very ageing. If you wear glasses. check you keep them with you! Avoid fussy strings and chains round your neck.

a) **Clothes fit.** An elegantly loose fit is appropriate whatever the styling. Trousers, jackets, coats, skirts and sleeves should all be the right length for you – not too long or too short, too tight or too loose. The fit should also reflect the right cut for you, one that reflects the angles or curves, the proportion and balance of your body. A jacket can fit by measurement but be wrong in cut – designed for someone taller or with wider shoulders or shorter waist. If you always have trouble finding clothes to fit even though you are a standard size, try other manufacturers because the problem could be the cut not the fit.

b) **Clothes quality.** It is not always easy to recognise quality by the price tag as some expensive clothes are rubbish and some cheaper clothes are excellent value for money. Natural fibres such as wool, silk, cotton and linen look better and last longer. So do fabrics that contain a percentage of lycra. Some fabrics from the polyester and viscose families can go dull and limp. Washing and constant wearing causes the surface texture to suffer from pilling (forming tiny balls). But there are high quality synthetics available, especially in women's wear, with the properties you would expect from natural fibres (see 'quality control', pages 101–102).

c) **Clothes care and maintenance.** A maintenance checklist should cover whether all items are clean, pressed or steamed, checked for stains, checked for perspiration, with no missing buttons, loose hems, unravelling buttonholes or hanging threads.

d) **Clothes age.** Be honest about whether any of your clothes are either worn out or out of fashion. Being screamingly up to date is not necessary or appropriate for a professional image. However, fashion is a reflection of what is happening in society. Being in touch with what is current is vital. If you've lost touch with current fashion, people will presume that your thinking and your ideas are a bit *passé* as well.

Shoes. There are still people about who judge character by shoes. A professional image means being particular about keeping your shoes clean, well polished or brushed, comfortable but smart and well-fitting. Too loose and they look like barges and slip off the back of your heels as you walk, or make an irritating clacking noise – a real turn-off to others. Too tight and they go out of shape and spoil your posture and your image and will also ruin your feet. Keep all your shoes in good repair, heels not scuffed or worn down. Rotate your shoe wearing so that each pair can rest and recover between outings.

Accessories. Consider their age, style, quality and suitability. Are your accessories in keeping with your total look? A classic style of dress needs good quality, classic accessories unless you are making an alternative style statement.

Jewellery. Whether it's the real thing, costume jewellery or a piece from a designer/maker it should be good of its kind and contribute to your style statement. Sentimental jewellery such as name bracelets, fine gold chains and 'love' necklaces are too personal. They don't make a strong enough style statement and add unnecessary clutter to a business look.

Underwear. Working from the inside out check that your underwear gives you an appropriate line under your clothes. Check for anything showing that shouldn't be showing. Visible underwear, except as a strong fashion statement, is not part of a professional image unless your business is to promote underwear or sell sex. The visible pant line (VPL) under skirts or trousers is not acceptable. Always check your back view.

Grooming. People who are successful and well-groomed themselves find it hard to see past poor personal presentation. Be ruthless about observing your own grooming and assess whether it is an acceptable level for the image you need to project.

successful colour schemes

Sure-fire colour schemes come from age-old rules of aesthetics. Here are some examples:

- Neutrals: strictly speaking the 'no-colour' colours. Example: blacks, whites, greys; plus in fashion terms we can add creams and beiges, such as pebbles on a beach, and of course navy.
- Neutrals plus colour. Example: blacks, whites, greys, creams, navy with a splash of strong colour.
- Naturals: any colours that you might find in undyed fabrics. Example: string, putty, hessian.
- Herbs and spices. Example: the soft greens and related browns, yellows and oranges you would find in a spice rack.
- Complementary opposites: combining tones of any colours that sit opposite each other on the colour wheel, such as blue/orange, yellow/purple and red/green. Example: blue/orange complementary opposite can be achieved with denim jeans and a peach shirt, yellow/purple opposite can be achieved with a purple jumper and gold bracelets, red/green, think of a holly bush with bright red berries and dark green leaves.
- Same family: dark and light tones of the same colour. Example: dark purple/mauve/lilac.

colour analysis

Some people have a good eye and can create interesting colour schemes that complement their own colouring. Even people with a good eye can find it difficult to assess their own colouring characteristics. If you are not sure about what suits you, arrange to see an image consultant who has been trained to assess personal colouring. Having an image consultant is not a luxury or a vanity. It is a necessary part of building a professional image. A good consultant can establish your unique colour profile by analysing your hair colour, eye colour and skin tone. A palette of colours will be selected for you that will harmonise with your colouring and co-ordinate with each other.

Looking at hair, skin and eyes, common colour patterns emerge. For example:

■ **Deep**
Black, dark brown, chestnut hair with dark brown, hazel eyes and medium to dark skin tone

■ **Bright**
Black, mid-brown hair with bright blue, bright hazel, green eyes and light to medium skin tone

■ **Warm**
Ginger, auburn, copper hair with brown, hazel, green eyes and golden or pale skin

■ **Light**
Blonde, ash and golden, yellowy-grey or mousey hair with blue, green, grey eyes and medium to light skin tone

■ **Muted**
Blonde, light brown, mousey hair with greeny grey, olive or brown eyes and medium to deep skin tone

■ **Cool**
Grey, white, ash, mousey brown hair with grey/blue, grey/brown, blue eyes and deep, dusty or rosy skin tone

People are instinctively drawn towards a particular colour or family of colours which may or may not suit them. Sometimes colours are chosen that are a closer match psychologically than physically and their choice is an expression of temperament and personality rather than aesthetics. An outgoing and sociable person might choose an orange-red in tune with their capabilities as a leader and positive thinker which clashes with their muted colouring. Sheer force of personality often overcomes these apparent mismatches. If you choose a small family of colours for your clothes and limit prints and patterns you are more likely to have clothes that can be worn with each other.

magic colours

We use our eyes as a powerful form of non-verbal communication. The most flattering colours are the ones that, when worn near your face, are in harmony with your natural colouring. One way of looking for a flattering colour to wear is to establish your dominant eye colour then either match it or look for its complementary opposite (see 'successful colour schemes' above). Men could use this idea to experiment with a new tie colour, women with a new idea for a blouse, T-shirt or scarf to enhance their eye colour. Like magic, it will help your audience to focus on you and what you are saying.

These suggestions for complementary colours are not always theoretically correct opposites but are visually harmonious. The suggested colour choices are in medium tones, so you can select lighter or deeper tones according to the depth of your eye colour.

Eye colour	Flattered by
Blue	Peach, apricot
Blue-grey	Rose
Blue-green	Rust
Green	Red
Hazel	Violet
Light brown	Turquoise, soft navy
Deep brown	Pine green, aubergine
Greeny grey	Burgundy

sensitive colours

The artistic and intuitive colours lie in the purple, violet, lavender and periwinkle palette. Just a touch of one of these colours softens an otherwise hard or over-formal look.

communicator colours

The whole range of medium blues is well received by an audience. Blues flatter a wide variety of skin tones and look good on television, for meetings and on a conference platform.

The secret of any successful colour scheme is that the colours like you as much as you like the colours.

primary physical characteristic

In order to determine how to dress appropriately to enhance your build, weight and height you need to decide which of your physical characteristics is the most obvious. Then make sure you dress it to advantage.

Look at the overall impression you give through your physical appearance – your 'personal architecture' – and avoid either zooming in on your liabilities or hyping your assets (real or imagined) and dress what's real.

- ▩ **Silhouette** – tall, medium, short, thin, squat, pear-shaped, curvy, triangular?
- ▩ **Weight** – overweight, underweight, average?
- ▩ **Colouring** – striking, bit mousy?
- ▩ **Posture** – upright, stooped, slouched, athletic?
- ▩ **Height/weight ratio** – do you look wide or narrow when viewed from a distance?
- ▩ **Health & fitness** – fit and well, a bit poorly, pale, spotty?

Common sense and objective observation are the key skills needed for this exercise. You need to look at the total picture you present and avoid the two most common dangers – zooming in for a close-up on real or imagined defects and hyping your assets. Decide what it is that people see first when they look at you, then dress that element to its most flattering extent.

lifestyle

What do you spend most of a typical week or month doing? Do you go sailing at the weekends? Spend as much time as you can with the family? Take work home? Are you decorating or renovating a house? If you are in full-time work you will spend on average 10–12 hours a day working and travelling, 2–3 hours eating, preparing food and household chores, 2–4 hours at leisure and 8 hours sleeping. Some people keep the same clothes on all day and just roll on from one activity to another: staff meeting, cooking chips, personal computer, watching TV, taking the dog for a walk, then all the clothes come off at bedtime and a fresh lot worn the next day.

Other people have an outfit for every activity. Work clothes are stripped off as soon as they get in and they put on track suit or tee-shirt and shorts or their special dog-walking clothes. Sometimes the strip is a symbolic gesture to separate on-duty from off-duty and sometimes for practical reasons to keep work clothes clean and in good condition and not spoiled by lounging about, dealing with small children, animals or household chores.

Whatever your life style you can't support it unless you work. This means that time, effort and money have to be invested in maintaining your personal brand through an appropriate wardrobe. Even if you resent it bitterly – invest in your wardrobe – you are investing in your future.

wardrobe management

The decision-making process involved in buying clothes usually boils
down to considering a set of polar opposite consumer choices and
applying them to oneself asking whether they fit our perception of self:

Young	–	Old
Male	–	Female
Work	–	Play
Conformity	–	Rebellion
Domestic	–	Public
Fashion	–	Anti-fashion
Freedom	–	Control
Display	–	Concealment
Indoors	–	Outdoors

Getting yourself and your wardrobe organised so that you
know what you've got, which are the successful items and
where the weaknesses are, is a first step to managing your
clothes rather than letting them control you. Very few of us
have the opportunity to start all over again with our business
wardrobe, or with our lives, for that matter. The sensible thing
to do is to make a plan that utilises what you've got.

the 'essential units' wardrobe plan

■ The most important aspect about the essential units
wardrobe plan is that it is *small*.

■ Every item should be carefully chosen so that everything matches. Think about every item in the context
of:

   Colour – Fabric – Shape and Style – Function.

■ Spend time identifying what are the essentials for your
needs. Build on these basic units. When you are sure
what really suits you and what works in reality then
you can gradually add further items to the basics.

- With care and flair, each item in the essential units wardrobe will fit with any other, like interchangeable pieces of an interlocking puzzle.
- Like most efficient systems, the essential units system is *simple*. The hard work goes into the thinking, planning and research stages. The rewards lie in the confidence that comes from the results of a well-managed investment. It is possible to look good on a daily basis with the minimum of fuss.

action plan

- Identify existing basics.
- Identify the 'gaps'.
- Decide on appropriate colour scheme – which basic neutrals, which accents.
- Decide on a budget.
- Plan a time scale.
- Do your research – find out what is available in your size, price range, preferred style, best colours, likely labels.
- Shop. Whether you are going to a department store or shopping by mail-order, set aside enough time to do the job properly. Follow up window-shopping with serious buying.
- Look for the right accessories that are going to add style and flair.

colour

- A wardrobe based on the essential unit idea works best when planned for a very restricted colour scheme. Two, or at the most, three colours that suit you and complement each other form the basics. Highlight these with one or more accent colours used in small quantities.

- Apply the same rules of a restricted colour scheme to underwear, jewellery and accessories.
- Colours can be chosen from your best neutrals, either light, medium or dark, for a conservative look, or built up from stronger, brighter colours for a more creative or informal look.
- Add from as wide a range of accents as you like.

fabric

- In temperate climates it is not usually necessary to have completely different wardrobes for the seasons of the year. In most cases it is enough to put together outfits consisting of medium-weight fabrics in natural fibres such as wool, cotton, linen or silk and put on or take off the layers according to the temperature.
- If the summers get hotter and the winters colder, you may have to consider developing significantly different capsule wardrobes for the changing seasons. However, the layering technique using trans-seasonal fabrics and garments will reduce the need for seasonal wardrobes.
- Contrasting textures are more useful than a mixture of patterns that cannot be worn together.

shape and style

- Each essential unit should be of a flattering style and silhouette. Every piece should work for its keep. You cannot afford any passengers.
- Each piece should have the capability of being worn over, under or with any other piece.
- Every combination should maintain a good line and flatter the appearance.

function

■ Decide what the units are for. Are they solely for work or will they double as off-duty clothes?

■ Each item in the essential units wardrobe should be chosen for a particular purpose but you will get more wear from items that serve more than one purpose: office, dinner, conference or presentation.

■ Successful, versatile items can be used to create new satellite wardrobes with different functions.

ten ways to make your business wardrobe more effective

It is said that we wear 15 per cent of our clothes 85 per cent of the time. The key to a successful wardrobe is to be well organised, have fewer clothes and be ruthless about the clothes that are not earning their keep. If being organised does not come naturally a few practical hints might help:

1. Look at the eight to ten garments you wear more often than any of the others. What makes them so popular? Once you can analyse why they are successful you can repeat the success and make fewer mistakes.

2. Look at the items you don't wear so often, or not at all. What is the matter with each of them? You probably don't wear them for one of these reasons:
   - it doesn't fit;
   - it's the wrong colour;
   - it's not really 'you';
   - it's out of fashion;
   - you don't like it any more but it's too good to throw away;
   - you are saving it for 'best'.

Don't let it hang there making you feel guilty for wasting the money, or a fool for making a mistake. Get rid of it. No, it won't come back into fashion and if it does it won't look the same next time round.

3. Have six-monthly sort outs. Get everything out of the wardrobe(s) and cupboard(s) and put it around the room. Keep your real favourites to one side and take a ruthless look at the rest. Some will be OK with a bit of attention, some need to go in a black bin bag, some could be offered to a friend or someone in the family who admires them. Consider offering the good quality, little worn garments for sale in a dress-exchange. This mainly applies to women's clothes but there are also some places for men. The rest can go to a jumble sale or charity shop (it would be a kindness not to cut off buttons or unpick zips).

4. Identify the gaps this exercise has left. Make a shopping list. Stick to it!

5. Try to recognise those mistakes you keep repeating and avoid them in the future:
   - the bargain you never wear;
   - the skirt that is waiting for 'when I lose weight';
   - the jacket that looked terrific on someone else;
   - the outfit bought in a hurry because you were desperate for something for a special occasion;
   - the outfit you bought to cheer yourself up and have never worn;
   - the tie that your mother/sister/girlfriend bought that you hate but keep because you don't like to throw it away in case you offend her; don't let other people buy your ties (or anything else for that matter) unless you admire their taste. Say that you have to abide by a very strict dress code at work and must be responsible for your own wardrobe.

6. Remember the *Rule of Three*. Before you buy something new, consider whether it will:
   - go with *three* things you already have;
   - can be worn for *three* different kinds of event;
   - could be worn for *three* seasons.
7. There is also the *Cost Per Wearing* factor – *CPW*. Imagine you have bought a suit for work for £250. You wear it once a week for a year.

   Divide £250 by 52 and you have:

   $$\frac{250}{52} = \text{CPW } 4.80$$

   You might at the same time have bought a silk shirt in the sale for £35 but have only been able to find an opportunity to wear it twice. The CPW factor looks like this:

   $$\frac{35}{2} = \text{CPW } 17.5$$

   Look at your existing wardrobe and apply the CPW factor. You may be in for a few surprises. Aim for a CPW factor that is as low as possible.
8. Don't be tempted by something merely 'useful' – it's likely to be boring as well. Only buy something when you can honestly answer 'yes' to these two questions:
   - Is it appropriate for my professional image?
   - Does it make me look terrific?
9. Don't be afraid to have minor alterations done. Skirts and trousers can be made narrower or wider and their hems are easily shortened, as are sleeves. The cost is likely to be only a fraction of the purchase price but will make such a difference.

10. Keep your clothes *visible* – you won't wear what you can't see.

wardrobe maintenance

Nine ways to maintain your investment:

1. Keep everything cleaned, pressed, mended and stored properly. You'll then have more choice and fewer panics. Air outer clothes outside the wardrobe overnight, other clothes go in the linen basket.
2. Storage: give everything enough room so that it doesn't get creased or squashed.
3. Hangers: buy the correct hanger for the job:
   – skirts need to be supported from the waistband, not hung by those little stringy loops;
   – suit jackets need a strong wooden or padded hanger;
   – blouses in fine fabrics need soft padded hangers;
   – trousers should be either hung upside down with the hems gripped in rubber or folded over a padded bar;
   – shoes need shoe trees to help them stay in shape.
4. Use soft cotton gloves when putting on special tights to avoid snagging them.
5. Allow for dry-cleaning and repairs in your clothing budget.
6. Jacket, trousers and skirts should rest and relax between wearings.
7. Any garment that touches your skin should be washed before it is worn again.
8. Allow time for washing and ironing. Be realistic about your preference and temperament. Do you like ironing or not? A dozen beautiful cotton shirts need a lot of

tender loving care. Pay to have them laundered or ironed if you resent doing it yourself or are not prepared to learn.
9. Have a clothes brush handy and something to remove lint, fluff and cat's hairs. Sellotape wrapped round the fingers, sticky side out, works well.

quality control

If it doesn't come naturally you may not have acquired the skill of recognising a good fit and a high standard of construction. So, how do you tell a well-made garment? Here is a checklist for successful do-it-yourself quality control.

Six things to look for on the inside:

1. Seam allowances should be at least half an inch (1.5cm).
2. Seams should be finished with zig-zag or overlock stitch in a matching colour thread. Avoid pinked seams or raw edges.
3. The interfacings should be smooth and wrinkle-free and sit flat against the garment without pulling. Look carefully at collar, cuffs, revers and pockets.
4. Hems should be finished with tape or overlocked with a matching thread that does not show on the right side. A visible machine hem will not do except in special circumstances such as a design element, on fine jersey or a full circular skirt.
5. Good quality skirts, trousers and jackets always have a lining, at least for half their length, unless the current look is lightweight and unstructured or designed to be transparent.
6. Try this test – hold a side seam up to the light and gently pull apart – if you can see large gaps in the stitching then too few stitches per inch have been used and the garment will not wear well.

Nine things to look for on the outside:

1. Prints, checks and stripes should match at all seams including collars, pockets and front openings.
2. There should be no loose threads anywhere.
3. Any topstitching should be straight and even.
4. Pockets should lie flat and be sewn on straight.
5. Buttons should be a good colour match for the fabric and the correct size for the buttonhole.
6. Buttonholes should be straight and accurate with no loose threads.
7. The zip should lie flat and be a good colour match for the garment.
8. If the quality of the garment is otherwise good but spoilt by an inferior belt and buttons, a quality look can be restored by replacing them with buttons made from bone, metal, pearl, leather or wood.
9. Skirts and trousers have greater hanger appeal if displayed with a belt at the waist-line. These are seldom of good quality so you get a classier look by discarding the belt in favour of a good one of your own.

budget

Budget is an attitude of mind. My experience is that most people spend money according to what they are prepared to spend not on what they can afford. You could afford £275 on a suit but resent money spent on anything outside home and family interests. I could afford to spend £45 on a new duvet cover and pillow cases but consider it an outrageous sum. The same day I could spend the same amount on a meal for two and consider the money well spent and without a thing to show for it.

As a rough guide, allow three week's salary for a year's business wardrobe. If you earn £25,000 it is not unreasonable to allow £1,500 for major and minor items.

People have different priorities and preferences for how they spend their surplus income: doing up the house, designer trainers, keeping a pony, running a classic motor bike. Whatever your priorities and preferences, make sure a percentage of your income goes towards maintaining your investment in packaging your personal brand.

build your personal brand by identifying your personal style

As part of a full life composed of many small, simple pleasures, clothes are at least as important as food and drink and nearer to poetry, music and painting in their ability to satisfy the senses.

Bernat Klein, textile designer

individual image

Many people I work with have an unfocused sense of personal style. They lack confidence about what they should be wearing and in many cases simply don't know what they like. They want to meet the expectations of the organisation but don't want to sacrifice their integrity. My clients are highly qualified, well-educated professionals. Whatever their specialism, they voice similar concerns. Women fear that if they wear make-up, are well groomed and dress stylishly they will run the risk of being dubbed an 'executive trollop'. If they make no concessions to image at all they are perceived as unsophisticated, lesbian or left wing. The dilemma for both men and women is how to find a suitable way of demonstrating individuality, leadership and creativity within the guidelines of conventional business dress. Most of us know instinctively what we prefer to wear and have also developed some sense of what is appropriate for different occasions. At the same time we are able to recognise that what we really like has been eroded by habit, laziness, the needs of the job, other people's taste or unhelpful or pushy shop assistants. What we don't seem able to do is mould it all together to create our own individual, professional image.

style sulk

A young finance director was trapped in the usual accountant's uniform of navy suit, striped shirt and club tie. I guessed that this was not his preferred style as he was so uncomfortable in it. He felt obliged to wear formal clothes at his level in his organisation. He was wearing what was required but was doing so with the least possible grace and style. I asked him what his favourite off-duty garment was. His eyes lit up, 'My black leather jacket,' he said. We discovered that he had the capacity for stylish dressing off-duty but was not transferring his skill across to his business wardrobe. He was doing a 'style sulk'. If he couldn't do it his way then he wouldn't do it at all. He couldn't wear his leather jacket to work, but he did climb out of the strait-jacket of his current business image and move towards a more masculine, dramatic look in which he felt more at home. He still wears suits but the cut is more elegant and the accessories more individual.

the white shirt test

If you asked a roomful of female friends and colleagues (women are more willing to play this game than men) to put on the same white shirt and personalise it with a few limited accessories to reflect their taste and style, the results might fall into these categories:

Classic. Collar open, row of pearls showing, tucked into skirt or trousers.
Avant-garde. Buttons left open, wrapped round the waist, tying the shirt tails at the back, cuffs left open and hanging.
Masculine. Neck closed, fastened with a small brooch or scarf, cuffs done up, cufflinks.
Feminine. Neck open, chiffon scarf draped round neck-line, tucked in at waist.
Uncluttered. Neck open, cuffs closed, hanging straight outside skirt or trousers.
Decorated. Collar up, large brooch at neck, clip on buttons to cover existing buttons, tucked into skirt or trousers waistline then covered with a belt.
Natural. Collar undone, sleeves rolled up, cotton scarf at neck.
Glamorous. Buttons undone, collar up, sleeves pushed up, row of bracelets up one arm, belted over skirt or trousers.

Most women respond instinctively and work with what's available to reflect their style. If you make the exercise more sophisticated and ask the same people to personalise a whole business wardrobe the less confident will go to pieces.

style preference exercise

The following exercise is designed to:

- ■ Help you to decide what you really like.
- ■ Analyse how appropriate your preference is within the guidelines of what is acceptable for the job.
- ■ Show how you can transfer elements of your preferred style to the required style for the job.

The aim of the exercise is to reveal your true preferences. It is presented as a set of opposites using the extremes of style characteristics. Opposites can live together in one person but sometimes the stronger style wins. The drab Puritans won an eventual victory over the gaudy Cavaliers. The Puritans wore a quiet style of dress with no colour, only black and white, cut on simple lines with no adornment. In contrast the Cavalier style was colourful, extravagant and highly decorative.

Figure 6.1   *Style preference*

With thanks to the artist Steve Best

There is a contemporary parallel in the war between the 'Voluptuaries' and 'Cerebrals' as Brenda Polan of *The Times* observed. Giorgio Armani is the leader of the Cerebrals. He produces minimalist, classy, classic clothes in neutral colours. Whereas Gianni Versace, was a 'body exposing fantasist' who insisted 'real women don't wear beige', and thereby flew the flag for the Voluptuaries. There are women who enjoy the extremes of both styles and after wearing an Armani suit (or

Armani style suit) in a meeting will flaunt their assets in a Dolce and Gabbano bustier and Versace jeans at a club. Which do you prefer – or don't you know? Use this exercise to confirm or wake up your preferences.

Personal style opposites

Classic	–	Avant-garde
Masculine	–	Feminine
Uncluttered	–	Decorated
Natural	–	Glamorous
Neat and tidy	–	Chaotic
Plain	–	Patterned
Neutral colours	–	Bright colours
Pastels	–	Earthy colours
Tailored	–	Loose, unstructured

step 1

Looking at Figure 6.2 mark a point that shows how far the strength of your preference leans towards one of the extremes. In some cases you might mark the limits for both extremes. Some people prefer an uncluttered look for day and a decorated look for evening. You wouldn't do this unless your tastes were extreme. Some people choose to be very polished or glamorous for work and adopt a natural look for off-duty. If you are a person of extremes and opposites in taste, dress and behaviour your chart could have one or more loops in it. You should consider the problems of value judgements – tidiness and the masculine elements have higher values in professional dressing than untidiness and femininity.

interpret the result

- ▓ If you sometimes prefer one look and sometimes another or you can't decide between the extremes, your personal style will lack focus. A straight line through the centre indicates the most boring, least stylish look.

- ▓ A straight line down the left-hand side could indicate an uncompromising, boring, understated look which on a woman could be misunderstood as being unworldly unless it's done in very good taste.

- ▓ A straight line down the right-hand side would indicate an alarming and visually disturbing look. It is theatrical and highly expressive and could be interpreted as the wearer being obsessed with their appearance.

- ▓ Strong personalities with bold ideas will have straight lines at the far right or left. They need to remind themselves that extreme looks can be intimidating and could indicate arrogance and selfishness.

- ▓ An interesting and expressive look is usually indicated by a wavy line.

- ▓ A traditional business look is created where the left side predominates.

step 2

We all have elements of all the characteristics to some degree. One of them is likely to predominate. Decide which characteristic is most *you*. When you have selected your preferred style, you have to decide whether, in essence, it is appropriate for your personal brand. If it is appropriate, there follows advice on how to project the essence of your style and make it consistent. If it isn't, there is advice on how to hold on to the essentials of your look so that you feel right but can adapt it to meet your business requirements. Read the following section right through before going on to step 3 in the next section.

primary style characteristics
classic

A model of its kind, balanced, formal, restrained, regular, traditional or simple in style.

A classic dresser often has classical physique and features. They are typically of medium height with even, well-balanced features, well-proportioned body and well-groomed. They cannot tolerate extremes and are conservative in both style and outlook. Classical good looks are needed to wear severely classic clothes unrelieved by personal interpretation. A classic dresser looks best in all kinds of classic garments and styles from an Establishment business suit to black leather jacket, Levis and white T-shirt.

Colour. Neutral colours, subtle colours.
Fabric. Looks good in natural fibres: linen, silk, cotton, wool, good quality fabrics that tailor well and hang away from the body and do not cling or reveal the body; wool crepe, smooth wool gaberdine, cashmere, fine-knitted jersey in cotton or wool, cavalry twill, fine corduroy, lightweight flannel, satin, velvet, subtle brocade, brushed cotton, medium-weight denim, men's shirtings and suitings used for women's wear.
Texture. Not so good in heavy or hairy textures.
Pattern. Stylised, formal, geometric prints, even repeat patterns not splashes or daubs, paisley in favour of floral, small to medium dots, narrow to medium conservative stripes in favour of overscale.
Style plus. Can appear elegant and well dressed and achieve an expensive and classy look without using the expensive versions.
Style minus. Can be boring, too conservative, not prepared to experiment with colour, style or quality.

personal twist

- Keep to classic cut and colour but introduce more avant-garde accessories.
- Keep to classic cut but introduce fashion or fun colours.
- Keep to classic cut and colour but introduce interesting cloth and texture.
- Keep to classic colours but introduce more fashion forward, exaggerated style lines.

avant-garde

From the French, vanguard; leaders in new movements, ideas; an intelligentsia that develops new or experimental concepts.

As a true stylist your first rule is that when you see the wrong people wearing it, you move on. You enjoy wearing what most people are not wearing – yet! You belong with the style leaders. It is important for this kind of dresser to wear styles before they reach the general consumer. As soon as the look hits the high street or preferably before then, they have moved on to something else. This kind of dresser needs an audience.

Colour. All-black or all-white always make a strong statement, whatever the chosen style.
Fabric. Womenswear fabrics used for menswear, for example chiffon or lace; fabrics associated with one use used for another such as silver lamé for a boiler-suit or rubber, horse-blankets, plastic sheeting used for outerwear.
Texture. De-constructing fabrics, shredding, slashing, wearing them inside-out, fabrics constructed from discarded items – bottle caps, phone cards, orange fruit netting.
Pattern. Either looking back to an era that everyone else thinks is ugly, for example 1950s kitsch, or looking forward to new technology, as in welded seams.

Style plus. Can be seen as clever and adventurous, can attract admiration from conservative colleagues.

Style minus. An extreme avant-garde style can be seen as anarchic or difficult and attracts ridicule or envy.

personal twist

- ■ If this is your preferred style, wear your most conservative look for work but make as strong a statement at top and bottom (hair style, make-up, shoes) as you feel you can get away with.
- ■ Play up the juxtaposition of unexpected items or garments worn with a traditional business wardrobe.

masculine

Having qualities regarded as characteristic of men and boys.

In design terms masculine refers to darker colours, straighter lines, angles, crisper textures.

Colour. Navy, charcoal, pine green, burgundy, dark chocolate.

Fabric. Gaberdine, flannel, fine worsted – any fabric associated with traditional men's clothing.

Texture. Smooth or rugged, not in between.

Pattern. Stripes, herringbone, tartan, Prince of Wales check.

Style plus. Whether worn by a man or a woman, masculine design elements are perceived as professional, sober and business-like.

Style minus. In its extreme interpretation, can look intimidating when worn by a woman or severe and unapproachable when worn by a man.

personal twist

- ■ Use a touch of the stylistic opposite – soft colours for ties and shirts for men. Softer hair, daintier shoes, lighter colours for women.

■ For women – make sure that garments and accessories have just a touch of masculine styling rather than borrow wholesale from the man's wardrobe.

feminine

Having qualities regarded as characteristic of women and girls.

In design terms feminine means using lighter colours, flowing lines, curves, soft textures.

Colour. Bold bright or faded, gentle, soft tones, all shades of pink.
Fabric. Black velvet, white lace, chiffon, voile, angora, soft silks, crepe de Chine, broderie anglaise, organza, soft rayon, fine cotton jersey.
Texture. Transparent, floating fabrics that use embroidery, smocking or quilting.
Pattern. Floral prints, small Victorian prints and patterns, narrow blended stripes, watercolour wash abstract prints, faded cotton chintz.
Style plus. Looks good in antique or period clothes, in romantic styles, fragile jewellery, lace, sashes, hats, soft bows, classic clothes in lighter colours and softer fabrics, soft clinging and floating in favour of crisp, starchy or heavier versions.

Style minus. Can be too 'girly' on women, too effeminate on men. There is the problem of not being taken seriously – if the clothes are frilly and fluffy so might the thinking be. Men who enjoy the feminine design elements of dress will find their style best appreciated in a female environment. Pink shirt, interesting texture jacket, hand printed silk tie will be appropriate in all but the most conservative environments. Crisp tailoring or minimal decoration can bring this look to an acceptable level of professional dressing. There is still plenty of room for feminine interpretation in hair style and shoes.

personal twist

- ■ Use a touch of its stylistic opposite (masculine) and use just one masculine element.
- ■ Make sure that every aspect of the outfit has one of the feminine design elements even if it doesn't go all the way.

uncluttered

Few things, in order, not scattered.

To take an uncluttered style to the limit means to go for stark simplicity, minimalism; removing all decoration, no buttons, minimal accessories; concentrating on simple lines and neutral colours.

Colour. Cool neutrals in dark, medium or light tones such as black, navy, grey, rose brown, taupe, string, beige, ivory, off-white worn to blend, eg cream/porridge/white or charcoal grey/off-white to provide contrast.

Fabric. Modern or traditional fabrics, medium to heavy weight, that don't flow or swing. Linen and stone-washed silk are great but they crumple and distract from the simple line.

Texture. Flat, smooth surface.

Pattern. Self-pattern, or no pattern.

Style plus. Looks contemporary, chic, European, intellectual.

Style minus. Can be boring, can be stark, message of no holds barred.

personal twist

- ■ Use a monochromatic colour scheme using contrasting texture for visual interest.
- ■ Use one piece as a focal point: single button, asymmetric cut.

decorated

Adorned, richly ornamented.

In its extreme form can be visually exciting or a nightmare. Every aspect of appearance is embellished. Women: hair decorations, slides, combs and a scrunch in the hair, earrings, decorated spectacles, chain for spectacles, lavish make-up, charm bracelet, wrist-watch with decorative detail, clip-on buttons, pocket flaps, embroidery on blouse, stitching detail, embroidered tote bag, bows on shoes. Men: shirt, suit and tie all in different patterns and textures, waistcoat with decorative buttons, fob watch and chain, cufflinks, patterned socks, subtle and clever when done well, headache-making when not.
Colour. Any.
Fabric. Any.
Texture. Anything with surface texture or embellishment, crushed velvet, devorée, wool, self-patterned cottons, Jacquard weave, watered silk.
Pattern. Anything.
Style plus. Interesting to look at, often wears 'conversation pieces'. Willing to spend time looking for the right pieces.
Style minus. Doesn't know when to stop, over matches colour schemes, particularly at weddings, for example blue dress with white collar has blue and white shell buttons, a white hat with blue veiling, navy shoes with white toe cap, one row of blue beads, one row of white beads, navy handbag with white trim.

personal twist

- Keep to a tightly controlled colour scheme or stick to a theme, for example squares, African, or flowers.
- Always have one visual resting place so that the decoration is more effective.

natural

Not artificial, free from affectation.

A natural type is typically of athletic build, enjoys informality and being casual.

Colour. Plain colours, conservative palette, 'countryside' such as browns and greens, herbs not spices, nothing to frighten the animals, nautical combinations of blues and whites.

Fabric. Natural fibres, tweeds, hand-woven fabrics, medium to heavy weight corduroy, chambray, brushed cotton, quilted fabrics, tartan, denim, Aertex, raw silk, gabardine.

Texture. Matt surface, not shiny or theatrical fabrics.

Pattern. Small checks, eg gingham, over-check, tattersall check, Fair-Isle, Argyle tartan, narrow stripes, small-scale paisleys.

Style plus. Looks good in sports clothes: sailing, tennis, track suits, gym or workout gear, shorts, tee-shirts; the very English outdoors country look – cable-knit jumpers, sweaters, Guernsey pullovers, brogues, Barbour jacket, wellington boots, cords.

Style minus. Requires comfort before chic, ignores the needs of the event or the job, therefore has a tendency to be under-dressed. The casual style that a natural wears so well, can easily become sloppy or scruffy. Dressing up for a formal event such as an interview or special occasion such as a wedding can cause anxieties resulting in the chosen outfit looking uncomfortable and unrelated to the wearer. Women can be shy about revealing femininity or uncomfortable about 'dressing up'. Men and women can look and feel uncomfortable in formal clothes if cut and texture are not right for them.

personal twist

- ■ Go all out for the country gent or Sloane look with all the details.
- ■ Well-cut hair in terrific condition that always looks the same and needs minimum maintenance.
- ■ Fresh clean skin, skin fitness routine, healthy look.

■ Give professional dressing a nautical flavour using navy and white. Crisp white shirt with navy blazer, navy loafers.

■ A navy business suit cut for comfort in an easy-care fabric that will thrive on neglect, worn with blue cotton twill shirt and club or silk tie for men, status scarf for women.

glamorous

Seemingly mysterious and elusive fascination or allure, bewitching charm.

A glamorous or polished look can be attractive, glossy or artificial. A noticeable style, some people give it a film-star quality. Often a dramatic dresser, they feel at home in the extremes of stark simplicity, or clutter raised to the level of an art form. The look is not easily arrived at but is born of an intense interest in clothes and style and objects but not necessarily in itself. Typically, they present an understated style touched by bold strokes.

Colour. Strong, deep and rich or white and pale.

Fabric. Plain, but of the very best quality or ornate brocades, cashmere, printed velvet.

Texture. Surface decoration, embellishment, ethnic embroidery.

Pattern. Bold geometrics, highly stylised abstracts, rich colourways.

Style plus. Always interesting to look at, can be relied upon to dress up for a special occasion, in a conservative profession can sweep in and knock the breath out of stuffy colleagues or clients.

Style minus. Worn with confidence verging on arrogance, this look can be intimidating. The wearer has difficulty making compromises for appropriate professional dressing. They fail to realise that what they wear affects others as well as themselves.

personal twist

- Already a highly personal style.
- Stunning colour and/or texture, simple cut.
- One piece of oversized designer jewellery for women.
- Extreme cut in conservative colour for women.
- Embroidered waistcoat for men.
- Hand-woven cloth for jacket for men or women.
- Distinctive hat, and boots worn when travelling.

secondary style characteristics

neat and tidy

Over-concern with hygiene and order in clothing (being too neat and tidy) suggests anal-retentive types. A perfectionist can be a pleasure to look at but also runs the risk of appearing fussy and obsessive. Neatness, tidiness and high standards of grooming and hygiene are expected from uniform and quasi-uniform wearers – commissionaires, nurses or air-line pilots. Lack of proper order in dressing, particularly in uniform, suggests lack of discipline or potential lack of discipline and by association lack of professional competence.

chaotic

On the other hand, too much chaos can be charming or alarming. A chaotic dress style can be a sign of a disordered mind. As an example, think of patients from mental health care institutions in clothes that don't match, don't fit, are not well cared for, odd socks, buttons done up incorrectly. This is usually for two reasons: *(a)* because they have no sense of what is 'right' and *(b)* the people who care for them don't see dress as a priority and ignore the link between dress and self-esteem. The stereotypical absent-minded professor wears frayed cuffs, worn out woolly cardigans, mismatched colours and textures and a variety of interesting stains on tie and shirt front.

step 3

When you have decided on your primary style characteristics, use the *Personal twist* section of that characteristic and consider ways of emphasising your preferred look. If it is out of focus, this step should enable you to make a clearer style statement. If your style is making too strong a statement for the dominant culture of your firm or profession, it will give you ideas for pulling back a little.

where is the best arena for your style?

Every profession has a set of formal or informal expectations about what its practitioners will wear. Every business has stereotypes or at least a series of working role models for new entrants to emulate. Large organisations employ professionals across all business specialisms from accounts to marketing, and catering to production. The dominant dress code can change from department to department. Where will your style fit best?

Occupations such as the law, accountancy, finance or management consultancy, particularly those based in the City of London or Wall Street, still require partners to wear only formal business clothes. This level of dress is required at all times regardless of who they are meeting and in whatever part of the country. A company with a creative end-product such as an avant-garde film company might need a conservatively dressed accountant to ground them and give them credibility. A well-established management consultancy working with blue-chip clients might need a more avant-garde finance manager to give them the status of creative business thinkers.

In the public sector, in the NHS for example, the dominant culture varies widely from area to area and specialism to specialism. NHS Trusts are encouraged to think of themselves as a business and be more business-like in the way they operate. This can lead to a conflict between managers who want to go along this route and established clinicians and support staff who see their primary responsibility as providing patient care, not to get done up like a dog's dinner.

Education and Social Services don't place much emphasis on dress although I regularly meet exceptions. Casual wear is common among hands-on professionals such as social workers. 'Visiting people's homes you don't want to attract attention or wear anything too good because you don't know what you might have to sit on – or in' (Ruth Randell, social worker). In this kind of culture, a professional wearing smart clothes, even at executive level, is perceived as slightly suspect.

The Civil Service is a huge and complex organisation with a complex internal culture to match. Each department and layers of each department have their own rules which are difficult for an outsider and sometimes an insider to penetrate.

In the private sector, each industry has internal standards of dress and it is not possible to make helpful generalisations, but if your personal style is important to you, you will always be unhappy in an environment that does not encourage personal expression.

who is the best audience for your style?

women with all female colleagues
In a conservative environment staffed mainly by women, there are plenty of opportunities for a daily fashion parade if the work itself is rather boring. In a creative environment like a PR fashion company a strong personal style is taken for granted and won't attract overt comments. It is the clients' style that provides a constant source for comment.

women with all male colleagues
A woman in a predominantly male environment, in a conservative business such as law for example, can either choose to dress like one of the boys or choose the 'butterfly' option. The female equivalent of the dark suit and white shirt worn with a tie substitute will blend in with men's business suits. Bright

The 'Ladder of Response' indicates the stages at which fashions are picked up:

Innovators
Make the new moves, create the changes

Early acceptors
As soon as they see a new idea, will try it out

Late acceptors
Willing to take a risk after others have taken the first step

Early majority
Need to see proof & reality before committing themselves

Late majority
Need to have long term exposure before trying it out, by which time it's nearly out of fashion

Laggards
Pick up the idea as it's flying away

Rejectors
'Over my dead body'

colours, flowing hair and soft fabrics will show up like a butterfly in a room full of moths. An overt, hard-edged feminine style in male company implies the female would consume her male colleagues in time of trouble.

men with all female colleagues
As the only man you can indulge in creative and interesting clothes as this is the best environment for your appearance to attract notice and provoke comment.

men with all male colleagues
This is the least likely scenario for daily comment on clothes and style, although man-to-man conversations are heard about best places to have shirts made and where to locate good silk ties when on holiday in Italy.

As a fairly democratic organisation we are not keen on the 'tall poppy' syndrome. However, in the section that I head up, what I'm looking for is a person's ability to number-crunch – so it doesn't matter what they wear inside the building. Although, they might have a problem when it came to internal promotion.

Jeff Evans, banking consultant

Figure 6.2 *Dilettantes*

Reproduced by kind permission of Saturn Press, Swan's Island, Maine, USA

lack of style – whose fault is it?
social trends

Social, political and economic trends undoubtedly influence what we wear. The world of work has been transforming itself from rigid conformity to New Age *laissez-faire*. There is an inescapable move towards a more informal approach to life.

The style conscious manager will be struggling to choose between looking like a tough professional, a caring laid-back colleague and a dot.com entrepreneur. There is a nice irony in imagining the neat full circle that may yet occur. Following the move to casual dressing in business, several charities were established to redistribute unwanted suits so that the unemployed could wear them to job interviews. The unemployed might find that a suit is not *de rigueur* any more, they need business casual for jobs in the right places and ignore the business suits, so the charity will have to give the suits to the destitute. The suitless high flier will have to get replacement suits. Then for a while the rich and the destitute will look the same.

Your personal style will work best for you when it:

■ projects your personal values;
■ is in harmony with your personality;
■ is compatible with your product or service;
■ reflects your role and status;
■ reflects your competence;
■ respects your clients, customers and colleagues.

Your style is a way of making your personality visible, a powerful way of framing and demonstrating to the outside world how you see yourself. Do not park your personality in the car park, bring it right in with you every day.

the fashion factor

Any new trend, whether it is in fashion or management theory, will have its enthusiastic supporters and its quota of the suspicious. Being fashion forward in your personal style will be viewed according to where your audience is placed on the ladder of response to new ideas.

By the time the innovators have rejected team-building, pearlised leather or personal organisers the late majority are just beginning to see that they look quite good after all.

Fashion interprets current social, political and economic

trends and serves up our own era in the form of clothes. Sometimes we are not ready for what is served. The fashion continuum might include at any one time Mid-America 'home-on-the-range', Principal Boys, Dandies and bandaged cadavers. The fashion industry offers vast consumer choice, especially to women, and so there are plenty of opportunities for errors of judgement. Fashion has always been an easy target for humorists from *Punch* to the robust observations of my local greengrocer. This means that the style-conscious have to brave the flak from the conservative and the boorish. Fashion editors are interested in what will make a good visual 'story', not in guiding their readers through a debate about personal style.

insufficient role models

'No style please, we're British!' Finance and law are the heartland of Establishment style; the power lies with these men so they remain sartorial role models. Or do they? Professional men have more role models than women but fewer sartorial choices. Traditional professional dress for men that apes Establishment dressing is comparatively static and varies only in small degrees from year to year and company to company. There are other possible role models – the Italians maybe? Italians from sophisticated cities dress well anyway. Whatever they wear, they make sure they are co-ordinated and well presented.

negative conditioning

Many professionals, especially those from academic backgrounds, learn that self-presentation skills are vain, frivolous and unnecessary. An intellectually superior attitude to clothes has resulted in a low level of style awareness. A lack of street cred means that they end up looking dowdy, uncomfortable or simply boring. They have no pleasure and no pride in their appearance. They are unaware that the way they dress is inappropriate for the demands of the more public aspects of their work.

Parents have a lot to answer for, especially mothers – and I speak as one. For some of us, our only concern is that our children should be neat, clean and respectable. We want to dress them up as little adults. In contrast, other parents opt out of an interest in their children's clothing altogether and from a very early age allow their children to dictate to them about what they will wear. Without supervision or feedback the result is style anarchy. Putting children into school uniform solves some problems but creates others. Unless they receive positive feedback during their early years, children's negative feelings about clothes won't have been resolved by the time they have to make decisions about business dress. Other people's taste can act negatively on a developing sense of style. When self-esteem is low we allow partners, shop assistants, parents, children, bosses and friends to undermine our choice. Habit, laziness, lack of funds and the needs of the job all contribute negatively to an expression of self through personal style.

I recollect very clearly being in the corporate part of a large clearing bank in the 1980s working on the media team. The dress was very much pinstriped suits and braces and I tried to match that male style with striped shirts, strings of pearls and so on. Not terribly feminine, but then the environment was all about big deals, big fees and long lunches. It has taken me quite a long time to realise that I like being me, being feminine, and I have significantly toned down the masculine look, although short skirts and any hint of a cleavage are out for me, even though I see women who are dressing that way for work.

Debbie Clark

your personal brand on show

Now you have built your personal brand it is time to put it out in the marketplace, project your values and make an impact in important business situations. People often ask my advice about how to manage important business occasions. Apart from wanting good ideas about what to wear when travelling, the most common dilemmas (and ones that fill even the most competent and confident individuals with uncertainty) concern making a presentation and going for a job interview.

First impressions are most powerful in situations where there is a lot at stake, prime examples being business presentations (ranging from one to one meetings to platform presentations) or job interviews (again ranging from one to one sessions with a prospective employer to a panel interview with a score of participants). It must be worth putting extra effort into these challenging business situations because the effort will certainly repay you. Even if you do not get the job or do not get the contract, you leave behind a strong sense of yourself and your personal brand. You never know when your name will come up again. In the end, the choice of how to present yourself is your choice, but it should be an informed choice based on your best efforts to research prevailing corporate culture, and clarity about your role, status and your agenda focus for the day.

> If presentation matters in life… in a five minute hit with no context and no personal knowledge, how you seem is all you'll be.
> Peter York, management consultant, *Management Today*, June 1999

preparation and research

Every minute you spend on preparation and research is like an investment in your success. Your existing experience, knowledge and understanding count, of course, but a new subject or a new audience or a new approach will need even more preparation. The work is never wasted, because the quality of your personal brand is improved every time you perform well, and all that research can go into your archive for another time.

> It takes 100 units of preparation to get one unit of presentation.
> Kurt Hanks and Gerreld Pulsipher, *Getting Your Message Across*

make a model of it

Is it going to work? How do you know? Make a model of it to see if it really works: that is, give yourself an opportunity to try it out. This is more than just rehearsing the words. If you have never used a PowerPoint presentation from a laptop computer before, then mock up the situation and run it through. Although it is only a simulation, make it as close to the real thing as possible.

being in the spotlight

No rock star, opera singer or after-dinner speaker would dream of making an entrance without having not one, but many, rehearsals: from a simple walk-through to a full-on technical rehearsal, not to mention script and costume checks. I know a

They say that fortune favours the prepared mind. If this is so, then obviously time spent on research and preparation before a presentation is never wasted. Key questions to ask yourself include:

- ■ Who are my audience?
- ■ What are their expectations?
- ■ To what extent are they like me, not like me, share my values, sense of humour, education, background?
- ■ What are my objectives?
- ■ What is my main message?
- ■ Can I get the heart of my message out in one sentence?
- ■ How can I support my message non-verbally?
- ■ What could go wrong?

typical business presentation is not Wembley Arena and I know you may not be the next Robbie Williams (or if you are, keep reading), but you still need to get in as much rehearsal and preparation as you can. In place of a team of roadies and a sound crew, most of us have access to a camcorder and a supportive friend or colleague. We should not be afraid to use them. Like a professional performer, you will gain enormous benefit from taking a pre-performance check.

I find the performance/theatre metaphor very useful for presentation skills. It seems that leaders/managers, indeed people at all levels of organisations, are more than ever ready to realise that it's much easier to act the part when you look the part. You build your personal profile in small incremental steps, moving from unconscious incompetence to unconscious competence, and each step boosts your confidence – the bedrock of effective presentation.

Andrena Cumella, Senior Fellow Organisational Development,
OPM, London

performance checklist

- **Role:** have you checked what your role or status is for the session? Are you there as the 'specialist', a departmental representative, a mediator, the light entertainment, or the fall guy?
- **Script:** have you re-read your notes and got them down to a manageable set of prompts, index cards, OHPs, one page of A4 in large type or whatever works best for you?
- **Props:** have you put any props you need to illustrate your presentation in your bag or briefcase, or if someone else is responsible for audiovisuals, have you checked with them?
- **Sound:** have you checked the sound level in the room? Will everyone be able to hear you? Is there a fixed mike or a roving mike, any background noise you will have to take into account or try to minimise?
- **Costume:** are all the clothes you intend to wear ready to hand, clean and appropriate for the tone and nature of the occasion, with spares in case of emergencies? Does your outfit reflect your role for the session?
- **Lighting:** have you marked where you will stand so that everyone can see you? If the lighting in the room is not good, can you get more visibility by standing directly underneath whatever lighting there is? Could the lighting in the audience be switched off so that you can be seen better? Could you stand in front of a white screen or flipchart of white paper to create more impact if the lighting level is low?
- **Walk-through:** have you walked through how you are going to get in and out, on and off? Notice what you might bump into, tread on or trip over. Walk through the route and feel the atmosphere and size of the room.

- ■ **Prepare yourself: physically:** have you got your 'relaxed but alert' routine ready and rehearsed? Know what breathing exercises will work for you so that you can centre and focus yourself.
- ■ **Prepare yourself: mentally:** check on your PMA (positive mental attitude). Have you got your personal mantra ready? This is a good one: 'I am well prepared, I know what I'm talking about and I have every right to expect that things will go well.'
- ■ **Get the feel of the audience:** metaphorically peep out through the curtains before a show to get a sense of the mood and atmosphere.

The 'porridge principle' is applied to how much your confidence affects your personal impact and whether you project too much, too little or just the right amount of yourself.

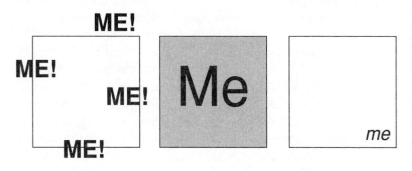

business presentations basics

Here are some ideas for presenting yourself at your professional best:

- ■ Remember that your audience is not an empty vessel waiting to be filled. All audiences come with their own sets of attitudes, opinions and prejudices – and a wide range of thoughts, feelings, emotions and values.

■ At a formal event, always stand up to make your presentation. It carries more impact.

■ Sit down and take your jacket off if you want to encourage discussion.

■ A well-defined shoulder line carries more authority, so keep it clear of hair and scarves and avoid fussy detailing. Wear a tailored jacket, and keep it buttoned up.

■ Choose an outfit that is congruent with your message – it isn't always appropriate to be booted and suited.

■ Avoid visual distractions to your main verbal message. Don't choose to wear anything too short, too tight or too see-through.

■ Check buttons and zips for security. Check for anything that might come apart from anything else.

■ Wear clothes that are comfortable, that you can move about in and will absorb sweat if you are an active presenter. A big presentation is not the right time to try out a new look or a new outfit unless your confidence is high.

■ Who do you most want to influence in the audience? Choose your outfit to impress them.

■ If your presentation ideas are radical, consider either making them appear even more radical by wearing a radical outfit, or toning down the message with a conservative outfit, so that you don't fire too many shots at once.

■ Check the background. Will you merge into it or stand out? A beige jacket will look great in front of corporate blue panels, but insignificant against light wood panelling.

■ A small audience requires a non-threatening presence, especially if you are all sitting close together, so over-bright clothes and strong styling will overpower the message.

- ■ If you have to sit at a table on a stage, especially in a short skirt, make sure there is a modesty cloth, or be careful how you sit and move when it is not your turn to speak, or you might give unintentional entertainment.
- ■ Keep current: be aware of what's in today's newspaper, the most recent play, book, film, and scandal.
- ■ Dress up a bit more than your audience expects. They'll love it.

making a team presentation

Look like a team by consulting each other in advance about what to wear. You do not have to resort to a uniform, but it is visually effective if you can agree on a degree of uniformity in clothing that underlines the team brand. For example, each team member might agree to wear navy, or all the women arrange to wear trouser suits on the day, or you could get a specially designed project tie for the men or a discreet badge. You can make a choice whether to emphasise differences in personality and expertise or show conformity.

> When we send the top team out to pitch for business we check with each other for consistency in image and check for any clashing or compromising colours and styles. What's important is to feel comfortable, not like a trussed chicken. What you've got on should work with you not against you and should reinforce the positive picture about yourself you have in your head. Then you can just get on and do the business.
> Jennifer Bowden, Managing Consultant, Human Resource Solutions

job interview basics

Most of us bring unneccessary baggage to an interview – emotional baggage, that is. We cart round all our insecurities and bad experiences, and the notion of engaging in the situation on equal terms seems to dissolve like sugar in tea. As soon as you open the envelope with the invitation to the interview, adopt a positive mental attitude. Being shortlisted and invited to an interview means that someone already thinks you can do the job. You have been invited to see if you fit in to the company culture, to test your confidence and personal presentation, and to establish how convincingly you can sell your skills, achievements and personality.

Most of the questions I get asked centre round what to wear and how to behave. The most common questions are:

- How should I sit/stand?
- What should I do with my hands?
- What should I wear?
- What should I say?
- How should I answer difficult questions?

how should I sit/stand?

Start by making a good entrance. Breathe naturally, shoulders down, head up, eye contact, smile, handshake. It works every time. Don't freeze up. It really is all right to move, to use your hands, to sit comfortably and to change your position in your chair. Cross your legs if it feels comfortable. Being natural and showing enthusiasm, energy and animation is more attractive to an interviewer than a flat face, no hand gestures and a rigid posture, which can be interpreted as a lack of connection to the situation, being afraid or being overly controlled – not qualities you'd want on your staff team, I presume.

what should I do with my hands?

Try to act naturally. If you are naturally expressive don't try too hard to rein it all in. Sitting on your hands either for real or metaphorically does not work either, because those of us who need our hands to speak with will just use our heads or shoulders instead. If you have ever witnessed this, as I have on video footage of would-be candidates, you will know that the hand gestures are preferable. Fold your hands loosely in your lap, or rest them on the side of the chair if it has arms, and if you suddenly notice you are doing a lot of arm waving you can return them to that position. In general terms, as long as the arms and hands do not go above shoulder level or past shoulder width you will look all right.

what should I wear?

Interviews tend to bring out the 'I've nothing to wear' in most of us. Unless there is very good reason not to, wearing a suit is still the safest option. Take some trouble with your interview outfit. The ideal outfit will give you confidence, reflect your personality, be recognisable as the company's team strip (so that you look as though you have already got the job) and support your personal brand identity. You could hang around the exit area of the building and watch people going in and coming out to see what they wear to give you a clue to the usual form of dress in the organisation. For manual or technical work, media or the social services, wearing casual clothes is usually acceptable. If you are not sure, ask the direct question. Ring up the Personnel Department and ask for the prevailing dress code in the company generally and what is expected for an interview.

men and women
A dark to medium-toned suit that is comfortable, flattering and practical is ideal. Black shoes and immaculate grooming are essential. Avoid boots, sandals and trainers. Play one wild card: hairstyle, glasses, cufflinks, tie, scarf, jewellery, colour combination – something that projects your personal brand. Do not bury your personality. If you are not working yet, the company will not expect a new or expensive outfit: a clean and pressed suit if you have one, or a jacket and skirt or trousers if you

don't, hair neatly styled and polished shoes, will show you are taking the situation seriously.

men

A shirt that is a lighter colour than the suit, worn with a coloured tie, is a safe bet. Two tones of the same colour for shirt and tie work well, for example a pale blue shirt with dark blue tie, cream shirt with bronzey coloured tie, pink shirt with burgundy tie. A crisp white shirt always looks as though you mean business, but can be unkind to your hair and complexion if your grooming is not perfect, particularly if you are prone to five o'clock shadow. Put some breath freshener and a linen hankie in your pocket. A predominantly red or predominantly blue tie are the conservative choices with a white shirt. Choose black shoes that do not have thick soles, no funny ties or socks.

women

Keep to clean lines and simple styling. A trouser or skirt suit is fine, as is a dress and jacket. The jacket can either match or coordinate with the dress or bottom half; matching is more formal. Discreet make-up and manicure that is not too obvious will give your look a polish. Have spare pair of tights, lipstick, breath freshener and a linen hankie in your handbag. Leave your coat, any shopping or extra bags at Reception. Skirts that are too short or ride up the thigh are a distraction, as are stockings and suspenders, dangly or hoop earrings, a low front and anything see-through: so no frills or fashion frighteners.

what should I say?

What questions are you most likely to be asked? Rehearse some appropriate responses. Know your material. Have an opinion but do not argue with the interviewer. Be aware of the hot issues in your market sector; read the paper that morning. Prepare statements and anecdotes that illustrate your suitability for the post.

The worst sins of a candidate are waffling, longwindedness, showing off and liking the sound of his or her own voice. The worst sins of an interviewer are looking or sounding bored, not being organised, being overly aggressive or rude, and conducting other business while interviewing.

how should I answer difficult questions?

What kind of difficult questions do you have in mind? The strategy here is to classify the questions, then decide how you will respond. Are they:

- Questions that you don't have an answer to but should know? Then just state simply that even though you have worked really hard at preparing for the interview, you didn't manage to cover that topic.
- Questions that you don't have an answer to which are unreasonable – how could you be expected to know? Same response: state simply that even though you have worked really hard at preparing for the interview, you didn't manage to cover that topic.
- Questions that probe into areas you don't want to reveal? Why don't you want to reveal them? Your CV or the application form should have explained any gaps or apparent discrepancies. Be polite, but if you continue to refuse to respond then you run the risk of making a negative impression.
- Questions that you simply don't understand? Ask for clarification – it's not an exam!

Honesty is always the best policy.

business travel basics

Your personal safety and your image are probably the two most important aspects of your personal brand when travel-

Interview basics include allowing plenty of time for preparation and research which will calm you and help you to focus on a successful outcome:

■ Arrive on time, with everything you need in a neat wallet or briefcase.
■ Arrive looking good. You never know who you might meet on the way in. Allow time to freshen up in the cloakroom.
■ Don't chew gum.
■ Always make an effort to look good whatever the job role.
■ Show evidence of top quality personal maintenance – top-to-toe grooming, from clean hair to shiny shoes.
■ Leave the flash jewellery at home.
■ Avoid overpowering perfume.
■ Don't advertise what you can't deliver!

ling. You can ruin your professional impact by arriving for a business meeting looking a mess or appearing strained, worried or frightened. You can look professional and well dressed without resorting to a display of conspicuous affluence. Your mobile phone, laptop or jewellery are so easy to steal. Avoid making yourself an easy target by not advertising them.

business travel basics: personal safety

■ Prepare for the journey and be sure you know your way.
■ Tell someone your route and when you expect to arrive. Phone that person when you get there and let him or her know if your plans change.
■ Have small change and a phonecard for emergencies in case your mobile packs up.
■ Always sit in the back of a cab.
■ Carry a personal alarm.
■ At the hotel, keep your room number to yourself.
■ Look confident and walk tall, with a sense of purpose.
■ Avoid risk by declining offers from strangers, however well meant.

business travel basics: image

- ▓ You get better service when you are better dressed.
- ▓ Select travel friendly clothes that have a Lycra content and will shed creases.
- ▓ Allow for expansion: your feet and stomach can swell when you are flying or sitting on a train for hours.
- ▓ Choose the kind of garments that will adapt to hot or cold conditions, formal or informal occasions, that will not attract dirt and do not retain perspiration. The effects of both after a long journey in an enclosed space are obvious.
- ▓ Restrict the colour scheme. Deep-toned neutrals like black, navy, or dark taupe look businesslike, don't show the dirt and can be dressed up or down. Take accessories from just one colour family, silver or gold for jewellery not both, and black for everything else: shoes, bag, briefcase, suitcase, suitbag, toilet bag.
- ▓ Use in-house facilities for ironing, dry-cleaning and valeting. Use your energies for business or resting, not wardrobe maintenance.
- ▓ Travel light, don't overpack. If you are travelling abroad and are unfamiliar with what is usually worn, then stick to your usual business dress and when you arrive assess what everyone else wears and buy what you need locally. That's what credit cards are for.
- ▓ Women travellers: take your favourite, shawl-size pashmina. It can do as a blanket, pillow, coat or cardigan.
- ▓ Only pack what you can pick up and carry in one bag. This means it stays with you at all times and does not get lost in transit.

on a budget? no suit? hate suits?

If you hate suits and simply feel that, like James Dyson, the inventor and businessman, you cannot do business in one, one option is to set up in business on your own, again like Dyson, and set your own standards. You can also look for a company that shares your philosophy on matters of dress, so it stops being an issue. If you are under 35, chances are you do not even own a suit. The convention of wearing a suit to an interview is still with us because it signifies that the wearer has taken the situation seriously and has made an appropriate effort. The only occasion when this does not apply is when you are being interviewed for a creative job where a suit would appear stuffy, a job with a high proportion of physical work, or when an organisation openly declares that their employees' choice of clothing is not an issue.

If you are reluctant to buy a suit because of a tight budget or you just hate suits, then try going through the wardrobe for a plain black jacket. This can be converted into a 'pseudo suit' by purchasing a black skirt or black trousers. As black is notoriously hard to match up, see if you can find a black that has a texture or surface pattern. Then the lack of a good match is not so noticeable and can look quite chic. Add a plain colour blouse, shirt or shell top. For men, if you are going for this look, then there is not an option on ties: buy or borrow a plain one. For women, a simple black dress with a contrast jacket will also do very well.

If this does not work and you feel obliged to buy a suit after all, then buy something from the middle of the range available in the High Street. Marks & Spencer, Next and Debenhams will have what you want. After the interview you can keep the suit for formal presentations and other business situations (see 'default business outfit' in Chapter 3), or you can split the top and bottom, wear the trousers to clubs and pubs that state 'no jeans', and the jacket will smarten up your work basics. Buy a pair of basic black shoes and keep them clean. After the event, these can also be worn to clubs and other venues with a stricter dress code. Black socks or black tights are essentials and can be bought cheaply anywhere (Primark usually have good multi-buy bargains) and can be worn any time. However, a cheap suit always looks just that – if not straight away, then it will sooner rather than later.

take action

A message for those of you who have been inspired by reading this to take action about building their personal brand:

DO SOMETHING NOW!

Building your personal brand is not an intellectual activity. You cannot build your personal brand in your head or by making lists, although for the tidy-minded that is not a bad place to start. Doing something now means now, not when you've got a pay rise, not when you've got the next big contract under your belt, not when you've got a new flat, not when the children start school, not when the children have left school, not when you have lost weight – it means NOW!

For those of you who are frightened of change, here's a message from Country and Western singer Tammy Wynette:

If you don't go out at night you'll never get to see the stars.

Finally, a message for those of you who are in a state of some confusion after reading this:

One must have chaos within oneself in order to give birth to a dancing star.

You can contact Eleri Sampson at:
Sampson Rees Executive Coaching
e-mail: sampsonrees@aol.com